Guardians

of the

Morning

Star

Structuring a New Nobility

Structuring a new nobility for a failing world enduringly betrayed by its political and religious leadership.

Author's Note

Guardians of the Morning Star is a book written in the
spirit of the ancient Templar knights, intended to reveal
the vast deception of democracy as a vehicle for freedom
along with key spiritual truths demonstrating
Christianity's fundamental flaws and failure to serve the
people.
In the light of the weakness of these crucial two pillars of
our society, 'Guardians of the Morning Star' explores the
need for a new social and political system employing
three core elements that have long been absent —
Strong and enduring leadership, a coherent spiritual code
and effective communication at every level.

Contents: Guardians of the Morning Star

Intro — Democracy Has Failed Us

In the first twenty or so years of the 21st century it has been proven beyond any doubt that democracy has failed us. Elected governments all over the world have trampled over individual rights and freedoms with increasingly bizarre Draconian laws, vast amounts of money wasted on armaments and war, business and taxation policies that favour the mega rich, poor education outcomes, poor health outcomes and finally with their insane responses to the so called covid pandemic.

These policies and priorities have one purpose and one purpose only — a purpose that many people will be astonished to consider and reluctant to face. The mega wealthy puppet masters pulling the strings behind so many governments have been busy orchestrating the transformation of citizens into little better than slaves; unhappy, unhealthy, afraid, ignorant, short-lived slaves for general use and abuse.

Slavery has been an enduring practise throughout thousands of years and having seen the undermining of freedom and the wanton proliferation of autocratic measures imposed on people by many states leading up to and during the covid pandemic, things are clearly not so very different in the 21st century.

There are those who might dispute that we're heading back to actually slavery so let's define it, simply and clearly. Three things define it. Are you free to do and think as you wish? Are you free to procreate as you would wish to? Are you free to own property and keep the substantial part of the fruits of your labours?

Over and above anything else, slavery is having to take part in things you do not wish to take part in and do not believe in. Another element of slavery was the ready castration of men and the rape of women. Not being able to earn money and own property is a factor less shocking than the above but it's still very important.

On the first count alone, in our so-called democracies, we submit to government all too often when they send us to war. We have no choice in the matter. It is always an executive decision and it costs us more in terms of freedom, lost lives, general havoc and economic sacrifice than any other action government could conceivably take.

That our governments get to choose to do these things is simply a bizarre convention based on nothing more than apathetic acceptance. We do not get a direct say in the wars our governments choose to fight and this is proof positive our democracies are complete shams.

On the second count, it has emerged post pandemic that our communities have suffered a significant loss in fertility, in part because of the now notorious side-effects of the covid vaccine that was in real terms forced on people, especially working people. This of course affects both men and women. Not even considering numerous other threats to human fertility, is it drawing such a long bow to count this as chemical castration?

On the third count, we earn money and can save to buy property so we can't be slaves, right? Wrong. If we earn money and put it away to save towards buying property but inflation eats away at it as quickly as we can save, are we really earning freedom or are we simply acquiring credits towards our food allocations as slaves? Every time inflation gets out of control, the secret ruling elite is stealing your money and it's all too often.

With inflation, interest rate manipulations and heavily eroded buying power through increasingly huge divisions of wealth, it can take a lifetime to buy a house, whereas only two generations ago, it took around five to ten years. We might willingly endure slavery for a few years to buy our homes but a lifetime?

Inflation is nothing new. It's been around for generations and many families who had considerable wealth several generations ago now have nothing, largely because of inflation. Yes, to succeed in this world, you cannot just have money put aside anymore. Independent wealth now requires vastly greater assets and is increasingly rare.

Every generation now has to perform, to climb the greasy pole or be locked into penury. We are wage slaves or we are in business but even if we're in business, once we retire, the rot sets in. If we're not actively pursuing wealth, it can easily leave us behind.

Some might say that's good — that it rewards those of energy and merit but what it really means is this: we are all dependant on government. That might be tolerable if those in government were clever, resourceful, kind and caring but nothing could be further from the truth.

Most of those in government are too stupid even to know that they are in fact robbing themselves. Stupid, incompetent, inconsiderate and quite often cruel. The perfect definition of slave masters. And they are bent, now, on whipping you.

Given the pitiful state of the public world that has existed for so long now, so clearly degraded in moral and intellectual terms, it was only a question of time before the mega rich and their puppet politicians made new and aggressive moves against freedom.

In the face of a disease that turned out to be no worse for the majority of people than a bout of flu, first world governments, (all elected by inadequate and highly suspect processes) took it on themselves to casually strip you of your rights and to criminally impose on you medical mandates along with a generous array of needless restrictions that ended up destroying lives and killing many.

They had no right to force anyone into medical procedures whether or not they were safe or effective. As it turns out they were neither safe nor effective. There was and never could be any justifiable reason to force any medical treatments on people, let alone these toxic, dangerous vaccines. It is simply not the proper business of government and if those in government feel it is, then they define themselves as megalomaniacs.

These acts of incredible cruelty and injustice were the acts of true psychopaths and they should never be forgotten nor ever forgiven. Yes, many people did die with covid or even of covid but seasonal disease has always killed many of our aged. Tragically, many have died from the side-effects of this criminally master-minded vaccine also. I can recall a seasonal influenza as recently as 2016 that was worse than covid yet nobody gave a damn then, least of all government.

The whole pandemic response was a deliberate strategy to undermine personal freedoms and make people slaves to their supposedly democracy based political will. Vast profits were made as well. It was the secret ruling elite's first overt move towards total, vicious control and will probably not be their last.

Bear in mind that politicians had already quietly done many things to strip you of your freedoms — surveillance, censorship, undermining free speech, criminalizing the use of symbols like the ancient swastika, drastic enhancement of police powers, pushing farmers around unreasonably and hundreds of unreasonable little laws like not allowing camping or driftwood fires on beaches.

So, if government and industry leaders wish to make slaves of us, the issue of slavery itself needs to be considered. If we are to argue that slavery is wrong, as has been accepted ostensibly for a long time, we must define what it is with some care.

We all owe allegiance to certain duties and obligations that could in a sense be seen as slavery but when our obligation to comply or conform moves past doing what is helpful or productive in the normal course of our lives, it must become suspect. With coercion, in a fearful, unquestioning society, cooperation becomes conformism, which is a terrible disease rather than a necessary aspect of society.

Let's consider the matter of war again. In the case of the first world war, it was ostensibly no more than a childish display of national bravado. Yet up to 20 million quality young men were pointlessly killed and nearly as many seriously wounded. The Vietnam War was vile — just plain wrong. Vast numbers dead and thousands of children deformed even today from the USA's use of horribly toxic dioxin laden defoliants.

Most people agree that the Iraq war was a mistake. The only major exception still open to debate is WW2 because of the issue of Nazism. Yet, however bad that might have been, the terrible, insidious decay of our societies since then must make us question who the true victors really were.

Factoring realism into the equation, just for one thing, the USA might have sold weapons to Britain but she did refuse to enter the war, herself, for around two years, draining Britain's capital reserves to the point where they had become beggars and economic advantage could be wrung from them for generations to come.

We would also do well to shed light on just why this was the deadliest war in human history with up to 90 million dead through a variety of causes.

Many of those casualties were civilians killed in Europe from indiscriminate allied blanket bombing, as described in Clive Ponting's detailed biography of Winston Churchill that revealed much about Britain's and the USA's ghastly involvement in that war.

Yes, the evidence is clear that the allied forces used criminal, shocking and evil tactics for much of that war, preferring to target civilians over military targets, given how difficult it was to strike these reliably. Millions of innocent, unsuspecting people were blasted out of existence or burned alive because it was *easier* for the allied air forces to target them.

Moreover, in a fascinating postscript to WW2, an ex spy, John Ainsworth Davis, under the pen name of Christopher Creighton, wrote a documentary style book called Op JB in which he claimed, amongst other things, that Churchill had ordered him to board and destroy a friendly Dutch submarine and kill all on board because the sub had spotted the Japanese fleet heading for Pearl Harbour. One presumes that if the Dutch sub's warning got out or word of it got out, there would have been no great loss for the US at Pearl Harbour and no incentive for the US to enter the war.

Creighton's claim was that Churchill desperately wanted the USA to enter the war and it would take an unforeseen, deadly, surprise attack catastrophe like Pearl Harbour to make her willing to do so. According to this ex-spy, Roosevelt wanted the US to enter the war as well but US public opinion had been firmly against it.

If this allegation is true, how can we claim that our leadership was any better than Germany's?

Ainsworth-Davis published the book in 1996, and it was never to be published or printed again, with the sub title: 'The Last Great Secret of the Second World War,

Fact or Fiction – Decide for Yourself', along with key documentation that appeared to authenticate it.

When you Google the book, the first entry is an Amazon listing for a paperback copy of the book for sale for $560, perhaps to discourage people from buying it. Fortunately, it's available at more sensible prices when you explore a little further.

The second Google listing is from the International Churchill Society saying: 'Op JB is a novel, no mistake, even though it is set up as "non-fiction" complete with photos and letters to the author from both Churchill and Ian Fleming ...' who was a British spy during the war before he became a famous writer of spy thrillers.

Who do they think they're fooling?

Wikispooks.com ties the loss of the Dutch submarine HNLMS K XVII after radio contact was lost on 21st December, 1941, to the OP JB account. It says it was assumed that she sailed into a Japanese line of mines while exiting the Gulf of Siam but that there was an alternative theory described by Ainsworth Davis in his book, involving him visiting the sub on a flying boat and placing fused cylinders of cyanide gas and high explosives aboard the vessel.

My research into mines is that they were used mainly in tight entrances or bays or they would not be feasible or cost-effective. If a sub had to approach a place like this they would be submerged and extremely cautious and mines were much fewer at depth, again for reasons of cost.

If K XVII was near the Gulf of Siam, she was thousands of nautical miles from where Creighton claimed she was not very far from Hawaii and if she was there, she would have been submerged as much as possible. The likelihood of her being lost to mines is possible but in my opinion quite remote.

Whatever really happened, 36 lives were lost on the sub and thousands more in Pearl Harbour.

In view of this cowardly treachery, what if the war really was primarily about supporting the European privately-owned banking system that Hitler had side-stepped, as many now claim? What would that make you feel, especially if you have struggled financially?

Did the US people ask for that war? Did the Britons ask for it (if you discount the absurd propaganda with which they were flooded)? In fact, many hundreds of the British aristocracy were imprisoned for having expressed support for Hitler. Did Australians or Canadians or New Zealanders ask for it?

No, their governments either forced it upon them just the same as war was forced on the German people or cajoled and manipulated them into it. Pushing war on civilian populations without their fully informed consent is clearly more about power and economics than about any care for people or their freedom.

And just by the way, in case you think that all that bombing of civilians in Europe happened as a necessary response to Germany bombing civilians in Britain, Hitler did not order London to be bombed before Churchill bombed Berlin.

According to Ponting, one stray German bomber dropped a load, harmlessly, by mistake on the outskirts of London and Churchill used this as an excuse to bomb Berlin. He had to do this twice before Hitler ordered retaliation. I'm not trying to excuse or laud Hitler but to shed light on just what sort of people Prime Minister Churchill and President Roosevelt were.

If there was a need for slavery — say to ensure the very survival of the human race, that might be different but really, there is no justifiable need for the average person to be a slave, at least in the cruel terms denoted by that word. No obvious external threats exist now that would require such emergency measures. There is a secret, hidden power that demands abject slavery so we should fight its imposition, not submit to it.

In all of the above wars, people were required to subordinate their interests to the interests of the state but increasingly it has become apparent that those wars were engineered with the primary intent of subjecting ordinary people to the demands and interests of the leaders and commercial interests of the time.

As for the Ukraine War, our supposedly free press has become so suspect now that I must reserve judgment on that until all the true facts come out. Even so, why not ask the people if we are to commit such vast sums of money to supporting one side or the other?

So, if you consider the concept in basic terms, slavery really does exist in modern times. By definition, abject slavery is a negative social condition that could only manifest in such a widespread way as it has where real communication in society was absent — and by a range of measures, good communication is currently at the lowest ebb we have seen for a very long time.

Yet many would argue that the way our societies are set up, we could not do without some sort of system of slavery without throwing the world into catastrophic chaos that would cause the death of millions.

So, assuming for a moment that's true, if you're going to have a system of slavery, why not call it what it truly is — a system of ownership of people. This is in fact the essence of what slavery is but in facing the concept squarely we can come to terms with the notion that while slavery connotes the appalling abuse of people, ownership need not. In fact, it would be much les likely because ownership typically elicits pride in people and who but a psychopath would be proud to horrifically abuse the people they own?

The word, own, also denotes qualities in a relationship between people that are more subtle and constructive than abusive and destructive. When we own something, we acknowledge it as a significant presence or factor in our lives. We own our families. We own our husbands and wives. In the great literature of the past, it was used in this sense of acknowledgement more than otherwise.

Yet, while we use the term slavery as a poor substitute for ownership of people, people will hide from the truth and vehemently deny that they are slaves even when they truly are. When people hide from the truth they are less able to shape their own reality, which is the core principle of freedom.

A properly organized and run feudal system could manifest the more caring and responsible aspects of ownership and leadership than any system which supports the lie that workers are anything but slaves. Then the system gets away with paying the workers a pittance while owning no responsibility for the many grave deficiencies that now exist in the lives of our worker slaves.

Modern slaves might once have had freedom from their masters having ownership over their bodies but have recently been subjected to the unjust imposition of vaccine mandates, effectively setting to nought the concept of freedom over one's own body.

This concept of personal freedom is thought to apply also in matters of sexuality but nine times out of ten a wealthy modern employer could persuade a woman to be his partner, temporarily or permanently. Many modern books and movies deal with this exact scenario and how many young women without means chosen by their wealthy employer would refuse him?

The difference between compulsion into sex through abject slavery and through the lure of wealth and standing is more to do with manners than anything fundamental. A slave owner or a business magnate get the same result and the difference is simply a matter of good presentation and manners — wooing a little instead of commanding.

So, in essence, many people are kept in the more abject form of slavery by believing the lie they that they are not slaves. If the basic communication processes within a single human body were so disrupted, it would certainly die. Fortunately, people in social terms are more resilient, although there are those who believe that the average person living the average working person life is in fact little more than a zombie.

While it is a reasonable thing to use the human body as an analogy to reach conclusions about the standards of social wellbeing, two things have to be acknowledged. The broader organism of humanity is more resilient but by the same token, it does not suffer in the way that individuals do.

Our current culture could even be completely destroyed and it would not necessarily mean that all human life would perish. Even so, our society is seriously diseased and we ignore the presence of serious illness in the overall body of humanity with grave consequences, especially to the individual.

With grave illness, if we make the right choices, we can still recuperate. Even if the human catastrophe ahead was substantial, many might yet live.

Yet in our current technologically complex world, no sane person would deny that catastrophic disease could also happen in such a way as no one survived. The mechanisms are there in such things as nuclear weapons and bio weapons research and they are multiplying through the machinations of our post WW2 coercive essentially non-democratic regimes.

At best, given the extraordinary circumstances we are now facing, logic dictates that we have some tough choices to make about leadership — choices about how we organize it and who we place in leadership roles. Tough choices and vital ones. We have to make the right ones to ensure our survival and our freedom. So, we all need to stop a while, take stock, and provide ourselves with the means to think more clearly.

Can it be done? Can we change?

The New York experiment of the First Street School in the 1960s described in George Dennison's book 'The Lives of Children' tells us that we can. If the subtle methods and thoughtful approaches to education of its idealistic teachers could bring about such spectacular change in a school environment, the same has to be true for wider society as well.

The problems may seem vast and intractable as they often did to the patient and worthy teachers of that tiny school but patience, persistence and true nobility can, it seems, achieve change that seems at the outset to be impossible.

Chapter 1 — What Stinks in our Leadership System?

It has been clear for a long time that almost every aspect of our lives indicates a change of direction is needed yet still nothing happens.

Why is that? Why should we just roll over, accept the wrongs as inevitable, and not try to avert an ugly fate for ourselves, our families, our culture?

A dying culture will bring the majority of people down with it just as it would be on a sinking ship. Just think how many lives would have been saved on the Titanic, had the men on watch been properly equipped with binoculars and had the captain set the right speed for the conditions.

So, in a way we are on the Titanic and we need a miracle – but what sort? Extending the analogy of good vision and preparedness, where good decisions need to be made, we do it with our heads and the head of our culture is of course its leadership.

Good leadership is the miracle that can do almost anything humanity needs yet at this time and in this system, one vital thing is absent from our system of leadership that actively precludes good outcomes — responsibility.

Elected representatives can and do wash their hands of responsibility for a number of reasons, which I'll cover in depth later but the key factor is that no one single mind or vision creates our policies and laws. They're invariably hotchpotch arrangements of random elements barely acceptable to the majority of parliamentary or congressional members. There is no vision and therefore no responsibility.

Yes, there are other factors but this alone means that the crucially important element of vision is absent from our leadership.

Does this really matter?

Let's look at life from an individual perspective. If we, as individuals, always made choices in life without relying on our own personal vision of things and sense of responsibility, what would happen? Most of us know from long, bitter experience that when we listen only to others and act on their impulses or directions rather than on our own, things go wrong — sometimes very seriously wrong.

When we consider things carefully, bearing the advice of others in mind, and shape our responses to the dictates of our own conscience and our own logical framework, amazingly good things can happen.

It can be strange to think just how much power there is in careful human thought. It *can* move mountains. It can build astonishing technology and it can free people from both pain and poverty. I like to think of the power of the human mind in magical terms and in a way, these manifestations of mental power are clear demonstrations of mind over matter.

As it happens, the principle of mind over matter applies on a socio-politic level just as well as it does on the individual. Yet in that framework, with respect to our current leaders, they've got it all wrong.

While worthy individuals regularly accomplish great miracles with just one head, the bright sparks in modern western style governments seem to think that many heads bickering away at each other works better towards producing positive outcomes.

Yes, many heads can contribute to the creation of miracles but not in the way things are conducted in the current mindless, irresponsible chaos of our farcical democratic systems.

Would many heads work concurrently on a single body? No, it would be strange and useless indeed — jerking all over the place and acting like some sort of unco moronic gadget. Well, isn't this exactly what our current leadership looks like?

They all bicker with each other in one place and at one time without those in different levels of government responsibility having specific avenues to contribute in the proper place and at the proper time.

Different steps or levels of policy and law making require different inputs — different teams of individuals but each step must only have one individual deciding the final input at that level. If more than one is involved, vision, direction and integrity are lost.

On the basis of that logic, only one person should determine the final shape of law or policy. Contributing advice and insight will bring pertinent factors to the attention of that final creator but he alone should determine exactly how it looks.

It would not be productive to discuss the details of this mechanism in great detail this early in the piece but I do want to make it very clear that I am not advocating irresponsible, abusive autocracy. There are good ways to ensure that does not happen, like instituting a just moral code and planning for responsible leadership. I am advocating more rights for citizens, not less, although the outward appearance of what we have come to know as monarchy would seem to exclude that.

In any case, many of us already live under such a system of autocracy without knowing it. We think that it's all fair and adequate protections are in place against rampant, wayward authority but as soon as you really have to deal with government, at least in my country,

Australia, you realize that most of those supposed protections and rights they flaunt are really no more than useless bits of paper.

In part, republican style government with an elected president does amount to a single person having the ultimate say on some things — yet it still has grave deficiencies. The checks and balances built into western presidential systems protect against extremist policies but they also prevent initiative and creative action.

Yes, even presidential leadership fails, in part because it is temporary and in part because the system of choosing leaders is so pathetically inadequate. Nations do not get anything like the best because of woefully deficient selection processes and if they did get good men, they would not get them for long enough.

If an individually responsible sort of leadership is to work effectively, the best leaders need to be found by more complex, subtle means and they need to have more time to do the job properly.

Just look at how the latest British PM was chosen. Richie Sunak was just another parliamentarian out of hundreds but for some reason he was chosen from a select group of around three or four on the basis of having enough votes, predetermined and publicly stated, without reference to any secret ballot.

Yes, apparently there is no effective secret ballot in the choosing of the PM in the great source nation of the democratic world! The votes are laid on the table up front and effectively only a few out of the whole parliament can be considered for the job!

The ballot is not secret but the power brokers behind the selection of those who are considered for this office, *are* secret.

Not long after that, Chris Hipkins was chosen in New Zealand as a replacement for Jacinda Ardern, who left suddenly under a cloud of unpopularity, post pandemic, without any contest at all. Fortunately, he was not long in office.

No other candidates stood to oppose him, apparently on the basis of opinion polls saying he was the most popular alternative, despite him having been behind New Zealand's shameful pandemic response!

Is this democracy? A vote for the Prime Minister should be taken from amongst all of the elected members of the party.

Prime Ministers have huge power and under the Westminster system, they are never directly elected by the people yet when they're not even properly elected by their fellow representatives, what have we got? Not even the semblance of democracy!

Good leadership does not come out of nowhere, as the current supposedly democratic leadership seems to. Good leadership qualities in an individual depend in large part on something that is currently missing in our culture — the certainty of a universal, coherent and comprehensive spiritual code.

In the absence of such a code, very few individuals in the world today truly have the ability to lead well with care and honour. Most of them are lawyers whose prime motivation in choosing that career was personal power and money.

So why do we get so many lawyers and fools in politics? The fact is, the current political systems of most western nations are very poor environments for good men of principle. People are much like plants. Provide the right conditions for weeds and that's what you'll certainly get.

Very few who do have the right character traits would ever submit themselves to operating within the futile and soul-destroying corrupt environment of our current fake democratic system.

Such worthy people operate best in a completely different sort of environment and when they choose to move out of their own private sphere of influence to achieve things, they're generally careful to mix only in ones that make sense.

Creators, particularly writers, inventors, engineers, scientists and architects are the ones who offer true leadership to humanity. Over the centuries there have been some great creators who perceived the need to communicate with sufficient depth and clarity to discover the right path for individuals and for society and at times these people were fostered and encouraged by organizations like the Templars.

These worthy creative individuals could see what was needed and have been primarily responsible for the gradual growth of individual human consciousness towards a new beginning.

Such people know that devoting their lives to great and worthy pursuits is well justified and, despite how bad things currently look, because of their commitment, the human race may well be closer to a marvellous new beginning than it seems.

Close, but not there yet because of what is missing — that universal, coherent and comprehensive spiritual code, definitely absent from all of the world's major religions. Without a truly spiritual code the system will continue to evolve towards allowing those of the lowest character integrity the increasing freedom to behave dishonourably.

So, could creators and communicators be effective leaders under the right circumstances? Of course, if the system was designed by them to make sense and be a vehicle for sensible outcomes.

Currently, most of our leaders are lawyers and all they seem able to do is proliferate mountains of useless, counter-productive laws and red tape.

Key elements in the social organism are missing because unprincipled men work towards unworthy goals in government and in so doing they seek to deny great and worthy individuals a voice, working to suppress any meaningful attempts to communicate the truth.

In recent times, these corrupt, disrupting forces have dominated. Consequently, our world is decaying and the ships of our societies are falling apart at the seams. An entrenched criminal class made up of people that do not seem to fully understand what they are doing has led us for far too long — and the consequences of their deceit are becoming alarmingly evident. We have given criminals the reins of power.

While these unprincipled men hold the reins of power, they conspire to increase their power and decrease the power of those who would provide good, healthy enlightened leadership.

These conspiracies can take many forms but in large part they use fear and suspicion to control people so that rather than talking to each other, we find ourselves divided against one another on a number of levels.

This allows those currently in control to exploit us and find ever more malevolent, conniving and destructive ways of extracting advantage from the suffering of a great many people.

Certainly, it is hard to face the reality of this appalling situation and while it might be dangerous to step in and fight the good fight, it would be far more dangerous not to.

Those who choose to do this must be sure why they are doing it and sure also that they will not end up being just like their predecessors. This is where the matter of a core spiritual code is so important.

I have no great admiration for Jewish culture in general but it has generated one great core leadership concept — anavah — a wonderful ancient Hebrew word that was grossly mistranslated in the Christian bibles into the word 'meek'.

Anavah actually encompasses all the most vital elements of behaviour in the critical sphere of leadership and it has broad social and individual implications. We all have to be leaders at times and we are dependent on leaders so this critically important concept has great relevance to us all.

Anavah is the Hebrew word that Jesus used when he instructed his followers so famously in the Sermon on the Mount. It was poorly translated into the Greek as 'praus' and to 'meek' in western bibles but recent translations have acknowledged that a grave error was made.

New editions have replaced 'meek' with 'mild tempered' but even that new translation is so far from the true meaning as to be absurd and the truths revealed beyond that will have enormous implications both for leadership and for people around the world.

Our whole Christian culture has been imbued with the righteousness of being meek for centuries but it's all so wrong. There's no merit in being meek. It's simply a word that describes a sad, ill-favoured unfortunate person and nobody should expect anybody to be that way. No one should aspire to be meek yet because of a stupid, lazy mistranslation we glorify it and create ill consequences every time we do.

History in this world runs in cycles of grinding repetition but with each subsequent repetition, subtle new changes can be introduced until a tipping point is reached and the changes build on each other exponentially. Truth, such as is revealed by the concept of anavah, heralds great change and once such truths are revealed, light blazes out in the darkness when least expected — even when all hope seems lost.

Given the clear schism developing in society between the criminal world leadership (that might have much to do with lots of people feeling they should be meek) and large numbers of thoughtful, law-abiding individuals, today, conflict is inevitable. It will happen and we must face it and prepare for it. A great many already know that the current leadership class has to be changed and the long experiment in fake, dirty democracy abandoned.

Some say that we should work on improving and bolstering the democratic systems we have but there are several key problems with this. People are bored by the current system because it tends to promote boring people who do boring things. This leads to a lack of will to be involved at all, let alone work for constructive change. But more importantly, the current system has built into it many ways of resisting positive change.

Something else must replace it and experiments with Bolshevik or communist ideals have been far worse failures than democracy. Their bloodthirsty butchery and mind control leave people destitute and societies weak and impoverished. In the Golden Thread, Miguel Serrano speaks of Alexander Solzhenitsyn's amazement that the capitalists of the US would bail out Soviet Marxism in Russia with huge donations of wheat after agricultural collectivism failed. We cannot afford any more such 'equality' experiments.

Many blame the new globalist autocracy on fascist elements but I don't think fascism is all that relevant. Its core idea was simply strength through unity and as such, in terms of principle, there is no great moral downside. In practise, communism is much more widespread and uses wealth as a tool even more consistently than fascism.

The downside is when a party or political force uses an idea to suppress the free expression of opinion and practical communism was defined along these lines when Lenin broke with Martov in suppressing the freedom of expression of normal party members, thereby creating the branches of the Bolsheviks and Menshiviks. This has been maintained by all communist regimes.

Yes, Nazi Germany suppressed free speech but it was more specifically National Socialist than fascist. It did also raise normal people out of poverty, which many communist regimes fail to do, so it cannot be equated with the modern Globalist oligarchy that has pushed so hard to impoverish the middle class, nearly as closely as Bolshevik communism.

A return to more traditional systems looks and feels better and will be so long as it is carefully engineered to be so. It is our best chance for success yet we must never go back without going forwards in some way. The past can provide a general model but the specifics must be determined to some extent by current needs.

Feudal monarchy was employed successfully for great lengths of time yet clearly monarchy of any type would not be acceptable to modern people unless the law was first endowed with firm, inalienable protections that prohibited any abuse of individuals and guaranteed their rights — much more effectively, indeed, than they do today.

Clearly, even those theoretical protections would eventually end up useless or hollow if not guided by a firm-as-bedrock guiding principle.

So, this is where spiritual values and a core code of behaviour play a crucial part. They cannot be ambiguous, half-hearted or unclear in any way and must hold true to a single, binding core concept. As such, they must be simple, basic and clear.

Assuming the presence of these controls and clear spiritual direction, monarchy could then ensure that all the decisions taken made sense with respect to a core binding concept governing leadership behaviour — and no better core could be had than the brilliant, liberating concept of anavah.

Anavah, in its true meaning, speaks of individual awareness and responsibility with unequivocal clarity and if we applied this general principle to leadership, policy and decision-making, we would see vast improvements in our lives.

As I will argue in greater detail later, anavah can be properly construed not to mean meekness or humility but vigilance or in more detailed terms 'you will lead and be closer to god if you are willing to see and be curious about your surroundings while having the initiative to act strongly on your perception of the dangers'.

These qualities of leadership — perception, vigilance and diligence — are innately individual and to properly appreciate and apply them to leadership we have to acknowledge the importance, indeed even the pre-eminence of the individual. Exactly what the communists do not want.

The processes of visionary leadership would work very differently to what we have now. As the point of any public policy is honed down to a finely sharpened tip of effectiveness, fewer and fewer people can be involved so each of those involved must give their best and all those others who were involved must fall away to allow an ever-smaller number of people to do their work unimpeded.

With ever reducing numbers of individuals involved in whittling policy details down to reflect the clear and practical expression of the vision of a single responsible, caring mind, policies that truly demonstrate care and vision could be created.

This way, acknowledging the need for a single responsible individual to make the final crucial choices in refining the spear-tip of public policy, it could be made truly sharp.

To an extent this already happens and to make it happen more effectively is clearly compatible with democratic principles of inalienable human rights. In some ways, employing a monarch to do a president's work for life is just changing what we call our leader. Yet, as I will demonstrate throughout the course of this book, a hereditary monarch operating within a well constructed and orderly human system could execute the role much more effectively.

In the end, only one person can decide whether or not the tip of the spear of any single public policy is sufficiently sharp. He is the one with the final say and should bear the responsibility, not just for a year or two in some arbitrary term of office but in truth, for life.

Why for life?

It's about upbringing. If our leaders are not bred in keeping with a core spiritual concept like 'anavah', a concept of enhanced perception, vigilance and diligence, to rule within a culture that actively promotes inter-generational family upskilling, social responsibility and psychological improvement, in truth, how can there be any real responsibility?

Responsibility means that someone has the ability to respond reasonably and coherently when challenged over their decisions. How can they do that without reference to a clear and coherent set of guiding principles or indeed without having created something from their own conscience and vision?

Clearly, relying on a crude system of determining goals through a bunch if ill-informed, biased or wholly corrupt yeas or nays, current leadership is irresponsible and we have to look to finding alternatives.

Bolshevism and communism have been terrible failures. Dictatorship is crude and having no grounding in tradition or in spirituality, invariably ends up being cruel and inefficient. Oligarchy can work but its successes are too random because, just like our modern democracies, it has never been geared towards properly choosing its principal members, and in the end, no one person is responsible.

A return to a carefully designed monarchy is an option that few will have seriously considered but were it well-engineered by strong body of contributors and were the main players both for monarchy and nobility chosen with rigour and deliberation, public policy could work far more effectively. If the monarch and the nobles had to adhere to a well-defined spiritual code then a monarchic system could work better than ever before.

At this point, you, the reader, will likely have doubts about such a course of action but about one thing you can be sure. If we do not find some kind of path to establishing a system of responsible leadership, there will be a catastrophic descent into ongoing war, suffering, disease and widespread abysmal slavery.

Whether such a descent into mindless violence would signal the actual end the world or of humanity one cannot be certain but without enduring responsible leadership, the chances of a generally bad outcome will certainly be far greater.

It is your destiny, my destiny and the destiny of our remarkable, beloved children that we speak about and under our current system we are actively being targeted for an ignominious fate.

Do you really want it go on as it is? Do you want to suffer from the chronic auto immune illnesses that the piratical pharmaceutical industry conspires to impose on you? Do you wish to be told what to do in every aspect of your life, large and small, work and play? Do you want the unfettered bureaucrats to slowly eke away all the fun from our lives?

Are you happy to expect to remain a wage slave for your whole life forced into questionable actions and then subjected to medical procedures just to keep your job? Are you happy to see inflation erode all that you've worked for throughout your life?

Do you condone that the natural world around you is being degraded with each successive generation, losing species, losing forests, losing beauty — until all of our world becomes like those appalling garbage dumps that many of our poorest live out their lives in, scrounging for meagre scraps?

I ask you these questions because that is what the deeply, horribly corrupt current system of government will deliver to you.

True leadership can only come from the heart, from the hearts of men who are perceptive, vigilant, diligent and always willing to learn; men who have been well bred and carefully trained to take on the responsibility of leadership as their life's work — not faceless, mindless, spiritless politicians and bureaucrats whose primary forms of communication are sound bites and memos, and who are elected without people ever truly knowing who or what they are.

The farce of democracy has failed utterly and life under its fading spectre will only get worse. Those in control of it allow some of its aspects to work but will never allow the sort of change that will ensure it works fully and properly. No one takes any real or lasting responsibility for decisions made now and the greedy upwardly mobile horde of politicians are simply quivering to take bribes from the mega rich in one form or another to do their bidding.

The end of democracy is impending. That is inevitable. The only way we can ensure that subsequent rule does not fall to the squabbling oligarchy of mega rich bankers, shop keepers and gadget makers now trying to dominate, is to quietly set it up for ourselves.

There needs to be a coalition formed of like-minded people willing to accept and adhere to a comprehensive new spiritual code. These people would then work tirelessly to spread the code in a social organization that would ultimately be so large that those in control of the current system would be powerless. It can be done and it truly is the only way it could be done.

Some of you might be unsure about the need for a spiritual code. You will have seen the terrible hypocrisy and confusion of the supposedly spiritual codes we were told to obey in the past and justly decry them.

Yet there are many good reasons to have and to adhere to a code — a comprehensive, well worked out code that provides genuine guidance and insight.

Later, I'll discuss the ancient spiritual code on which many of our societies have been based and explore it with reference to integrity. I'll also examine how it became so corrupted and confused. Beyond that, I'll introduce the blueprint for a new code.

Chapter 2 — Bones of the Christian Spiritual Code

I have introduced the topic of the need for a new, effective spiritual code. The question on most people's lips will be, 'why *do* we need a spiritual code at all?' Is there really even such a thing as spirit?

While this is a subtle, complex matter central to the question of leadership I understand people having their doubts. Even so, I feel confident that I can demonstrate to you the vital importance and relevance of spirit. I ask you only to fairly and reasonably consider the elements as I present them. Along the way I will deal with spirit in all its many facets and believe that when the full case has been presented to you, both its existence and its relevance will be confirmed.

For now, it is enough to accept that a code is required for a number of clear and cogent reasons. Any major project follows some sort of code — building a house, setting up communications systems or conducting a medical procedure.

A widely shared code facilitates the social body of nations by creating a strong bond of understanding. As individuals, a code will give us a clear guide in our life decisions and provides us with both the joy and the confidence born of knowing who we are because we know what we stand for.

Yet we must face the uncomfortable fact that we had a code which failed us in the end. Each and every empire that espoused Judeo Christianity or Islam, became corrupt and destructive over time.

It is simply a wrong standpoint, particularly for our Caucasian culture and people.

In his 'The Golden Thread', Miguel Serrano talks passionately about Christianity being a Semitic/lunar, female conception compared to the individualistic, virile, solar Nordic conception of religion and philosophy which served us so well for so long.

He says of the Semitic/lunar: 'It leads directly to communism, where the heroic sense of life has no place and the sacrifice of today is always for a tomorrow that never comes, as in Christianity.

'All upon the altar stone of the amorphous, of the collective ... of the matriarchal number, of the millions of spermatozoa that reproduce without name and without destiny. The awful bureaucracy, the slavery at the end of the road. The democracy that exalts the average, the average word, average information, the standardization against all greatness, against all creative originality.'

Serrano does not always write clearly but in these passages, great passion seems to drive him. Yet clearly, not all Jews or Christians are communists. I believe Serrano is talking in general terms of trends about which the informed must make themselves aware and it has to be acknowledged that over the years, a great deal of support for communism, both in terms of ideas and of money, has come from the Jews.

Most recently, the British showed excellent potential for forging a great, enduring and honourable empire but in the end, it slipped away through their fingers. Christianity was one of the core pillars of the British empire but of what importance is it now? Its supposed ethos of caring now looks over a landscape of destruction and conformist misery.

As with empires before it, in large part it failed because the code of Christianity is inadequate, self-contradictory and fundamentally incoherent. It raved and it berated but its clearest and most cogent instructions were largely ignored.

The tired old Judeo-Christian value system has always been conflicted in many ways but was also not nearly specific enough in others. That probably made the citizens of the empire prone to looking backwards rather than forwards, to the negative instead of the positive and to the setting sun instead of the rising one. That code is too random and flawed to salvage.

By contrast the pagan idea of eternal rejuvenation, as opposed to a slow decay towards degradation and long-awaited intervention by a haughty vengeful god, is both beautiful and true.

Yet who can have dispute with the basic rules of the Ten Commandments given to Moses on Mount Sinai? Do not murder, do not steal, do not commit adultery, do not covet, respect your mother and father and the like. All very reasonable.

When Jesus spoke on a different mount much later (likely Mt Eremos), he provided other truths of about the same number — but the truths were not so much hard rules as general guidance; advice about priorities and about attitude. Yes, it seemed he believed that as time went by, lives became more complex and more advice was required.

Jesus pointedly gave the beatitudes to his followers on a mountain, probably to indicate that they were key contributions to spiritual thought next in importance only to his god's. Time had gone by and a more complex, subtle message was needed.

When he says, blessed are the poor, in spirit, because they shall inherit the kingdom of heaven (it cannot be the 'poor in spirit' without the comma, because spirit is what we need to value and cultivate in ourselves) he is not saying they will get an equal prize to those who are persecuted because of their righteousness. He is simply saying that there are more important things than money (namely spirit) and that we should not prioritise money over spirit.

This is all very well but have any of the major churches stood by that ethos?

Of all the beatitudes, 'the anav shall inherit the earth' stands out as the core element of his spiritual standpoint, firstly because it speaks about the most subtle and powerful quality that will be rewarded (anavah) and secondly because the reward for manifesting that quality is more substantial and specific.

All the just and worthy will experience the kingdom of heaven and be comforted by god and so on but only a few can inherit the earth. These people will ultimately be the leaders of the manifest world here on Earth and they will need the skills of leaders, perception, vigilance and diligence, not those of followers. Again, these are great sentiments but have we seen many leaders with these admirable qualities?

At least in some of the beatitudes, Jesus quoted from what he considered the most relevant of the ancient writings of his people in the ancient psalms and the like. This concept of 'anavah' was not new. It came directly from ancient writings and reputedly from the allegedly divine presence 'YHWH' before that.

On his mount, Mount Eremos, other than giving the beatitudes and elaborating on the commandments, Jesus gave both general and specific advice on behaviour, the most specific of which involved how to perform spiritual acts like giving alms, fasting and praying.

With prayer, he tells us clearly and unequivocally that it is a private act between us and god, so private that we should only do it in our bedrooms with the door shut! Yes, he unequivocally specifies the door being shut. Yet all the major religions advocate praying in public and often laud their financial benefactors, at least indirectly.

While all of the Judeo-Christian religions have become overly complex, corrupt and lost their way, some positive foundations of truth and justice are there in their most ancient writings. Clearly there is great value in the basics of the ancient religions and we would do well not to 'throw baby out with the bathwater' but there had to be something not quite right about them for all these wonderful truths to be so flagrantly ignored.

Simply speaking, the code came from ancient minds who lived in a primitive society where even the most learned had only the most limited literary resources and probably wrote very little. It was beyond them to create a code that took into account a sufficient number of elements to guide the modern world.

The spiritual value of Anavah is because it is not a doctrine or a religion but above all a great core idea. Yet can a tree survive with leaves and trunk alone? No, it needs roots as well and as they say, the devil is in the detail — or perhaps in the absence of it.

Anavah is a powerful concept but it draws its value not from any claim of authenticity or contractual clan ownership of divine insight but from its truth and its utility.

Its essence is that we should be aware and think for ourselves and Jesus reflects this when he advises us to pray alone with the door shut, in the sight of god.

Incidentally, this being who gave the insight of the concept of anavah was clearly not interested in granting ownership of a monopoly on his power and influence. He gave his name as Yahweh, which has been translated (also incorrectly) as 'I am that I am', and at the very least we can see this as a polite refusal to provide a name that would give Moses ownership of him.

The true meaning of Yahweh is actually 'the divine singularity becoming the manifest' and sounds much more like a function or mission than a personal name. It is as if this being were saying to Moses, 'you don't need to know my name. It is enough that I am here (in great glory) and talking to you.

I believe I am right about this but clearly, a number of different interpretations could be made around that key statement. Most importantly, this series of Hebrew letters, letters that amount to a sentence in modern languages, is a statement of role or function more like 'King' than 'Richard'.

Any god or even any competent starship captain, if it came to that, would have to have known that the more evidence of his identity he gave to a primitive being, the more power this would give that primitive to manipulate others and treat them wrongfully. 'I'm on a first name basis with God so you have to do what I say,' would be a standpoint entirely counter-productive to a higher benevolent being's intent if he wished those under his care to be perceptive, vigilant and diligent, not to mention communicative.

Furthermore, such ownership of a name or any earthly definition of a god would ultimately lead to warlike divisions amongst the different peoples with all their different languages — as it has, because we have used this statement of 'YHWH' as a name — a name that confers ownership.

Yes, all the religions that sprang from this communication with Moses lost the point, advocating conformism and obedience rather than perception and vigilance, and therein did exactly what this guiding being did not want. Perhaps this, in the face of such obstinance and wilful misunderstanding, is why this god or more advanced being no longer bothers to communicate directly with humanity.

Moses was given the just and coherent code of the ten commandments and this, along with other crucial elements such as Greek influences like Plato, in the end led to great order, ultimately manifesting in such powers as the British Empire, so widespread across the globe that it was known to many as The Empire of the Never Setting Sun.

Some of the basics of the code were right as far as they went but inevitably religious and political leaders meddled with it and changed it out of expediency — as they did when they altered the commandment not to swear to a known falsehood in the name of god and turned it into 'you shall not use the name of god lightly' in the manner of cussing or bad language.

No doubt the leaders of the time did not wish to break a commandment when they lied to each other while swearing by god's name that it was the honest truth but all this convenient alteration does lead to some confusion about intent.

The fact is, all those who follow a code, leaders or otherwise, need to know the logical reasons why they should follow it. Christianity, however, has almost always taken a paternalistic attitude towards its followers and demanded that its doctrines and tenets be accepted without question. It has been impatient with questioning no doubt because it did not have the answers.

And how could it when it has always maintained that Jesus Christ will return again sometime in the future in a blaze of glory? The bible itself says that those events would occur before all those now alive (at the time of writing) were dead. (Matthew 16:28, 24:34)

Some of the basic philosophy of Christianity is good but pretty much all of the things it uses to maintain its position of power are wrongful and deceptive. This is because its principal guiding source, the Bible, is a broad collection of ancient middle eastern philosophical ideas the inclusions of which were largely determined by the murderous Roman Emperor Constantine. As such it is not and never was a code of divine insight and instruction.

So, in the light of its many inconsistencies, to any reasonable mind the logic wears thin.

In the end, the British, in many ways subject to this confused and poorly expressed code, gave up control of their world to those who dominated money and did so for no cogent reason.

The British empire foolishly gave power to those who had money rather than giving money to those who had natural charismatic power based on their love of life and true regard for their fellow man. Owing to that, the world is now threatened by a greedy hegemony of evil unlike any that has come before it.

Under the guise of commercial traders today are a set of cold minds with no regard for advancement of any kind, not spiritual, not intellectual, not emotional and in many cases not even financial. Their only aim is to throw down humanity under total control and they clearly have no will to promote divine will or real communication of any kind at any level.

Such a lack of compassion and goodwill is much like a dark, dull cloud creeping across the sky, a cloud that drowns out light, happiness and hope.

This cloud of the deluded mega rich uses money in the bluntest and most brutal ways to achieve its dark ends. It undermines the psyche of the young, destroys the health of many by diverse means and confuses the working population with futile so-called progressive viewpoints whose underlying message is not really equality or fairness. Instead, they espouse submission to group will and self-sacrifice for the benefit of the mythical 'many'.

Well, the fact is there is no 'many'. We are all individuals with our own individual needs and priorities; needs that are usually satisfied quite well in the absence of government meddling.

For some time, we have been fooled by those scheming for social decay into thinking we owe the many some sort of debt — some sort of vague responsibility for things we are simply not responsible for, things that we did not cause or benefit from in any way. They try to make us feel guilty but we are innocent.

Indeed, they are the ones that are guilty. The supposedly progressive Globalists behind this mythical many owe *us* big time. War is being waged on us now by scheming, covert elements frequently of great wealth and these elements are essentially Bolshevik or communist in nature.

Whatever it is, whatever it calls itself — communist, fascist, conservative, liberal or democrat — it is in fact communist if it places the good of the purely theoretical many over the good of the actual individual, especially if they try to make people feel guilty or regretful about themselves over matters they cannot control along the way.

Democracy simply cannot hold its own against these forces and unless we are to become ever more subject to these bloodthirsty fiends — for indeed they are no less than that — we need the bare, honest bones of an essential spiritual code and we need the decisive, worthy, responsible, pointy-ended leadership that will come from the clear understanding of it.

Chapter 3 — Why We Need to Have a Noble Class

In my introduction, I pointed out that we are in fact already at war, albeit a relatively covert one. So, if we are to properly deal with the realities of this war, we must know more about the enemy and their tactics and we must develop our own. Once we have worked that out, it will not be so very hard to respond and effectively deal with those who wrong us.

The key observation here is that the war is being waged on two fronts. We have seen communism by stealth imposing corrupt change on our populations most insidiously in a variety of ways but this is essentially a spiritual war or more accurately a war on the spirit because without indoctrination, propaganda and various other even more subtle means of mind control, they simply could not destroy us.

Without the gradual, ongoing suppression of the majority of our natural instincts, impulses and loyalties, the enemy would have no chance. To fight this and turn this around we need a coordinated body of people to guide our response. In fact, we need an informed and compassionate core class — a true nobility, a class traditionally known from ancient times as Guardians of the Morning Star.

The threat they would have to deal with may be relatively covert but every now and then, the ongoing war takes on a more material dimension. Every so often when a nation looks like freeing itself from the tentacles of corruption, the ongoing spiritual war erupts into a physical one in which the lives of millions are shattered along with vast tracts of natural lands and oceans.

This is why we need an organized, intelligent, well-trained and vigilant protective class. It is not enough simply to be aware of the covert war. We may well be able to protect ourselves and our families from the worst harm for a while but if our society fails, in the end we might all be doomed.

A mindless, conformist majority can turn on a minority, however clever or in-the-right they are. And how many times have our peoples been turned out of their homes to fight terrible wars that they should have had no interest in? It has all happened before and it will all happen again if we do not organize ourselves to fight the hidden enemy.

No sane individual would truly want to participate in any war ordered by a suspect leadership. After all, who benefits? You or me? No, clearly only the very few malign mega rich manipulators benefit.

People have to be already half destroyed by ongoing spiritual and psychological sabotage before they could even contemplate being involved in such a thing. Yet there are many like that now, so we do have to be prepared to protect ourselves if our attempts to forestall the broad sabotage of social consciousness fail.

We desperately need the establishment of a new, noble knighthood to begin the process of banishing this dark, toxic cloud that manifests in our time — principally as the communist globalist reset.

To do this properly, those involved will need to understand that deceit is the tool of the enemy. We also need to understand that deceit is one of the worst sorts of crimes. Consequently, the architects of this new knighthood will need to focus on discovery and adherence to the most fundamental spiritual truths to guide them in the ways of the light.

Interest in and concern for the spiritual is the pure opposite of dark deceit and it is the only way to truly free ourselves from it, in immediate pragmatic terms, to free ourselves from the domination of the psychopaths who dominate through money. A tainted spirit seeks material security and power above all else while a pure one seeks knowledge, enlightening experience and genuine, loyal friendships.

Traditionally, knights were not simply active, powerful men but were intelligent and often deeply spiritual as well. The Templars of 13ᵗʰ and 14ᵗʰ Century Europe were certainly that but they were also committed to helping people in very practical ways as well and were good proof of the principle that a noble class can be good for society. These knights created great wealth through creating a safe banking system for travellers and traders and used this wealth to support the community.

Miguel Serrano, who concerned himself deeply with noble cultures of the past in his works, wrote much about these able, noble knights in his 'The Golden Thread' and observed for one thing, that the peasants did not pay tithes to the Templars when they were landowners. These spiritual knights organized the lives of many people without personal profit to themselves and cultivated a caste system that was largely free of hate and envy.

Serrano elaborates in the following observation.

'For the inhabitants of the Kali Yuga, belonging to a society, to a civitas atomized into classes and not into an initiatic varna, it is impossible to understand the world of castes of the past, organized upon the basis of distinct initiations, which would not hate or envy each other, because each of them would correspond to a wisdom and a magical penetration of "their universe." The farmer possessed his own initiatic secrets, of which he felt himself custodian by cosmic tradition. The same would occur with the worker, or rather, the transformer of matter, the builder.
'None was superior to the other; they completed each other.'

He goes on to draw a comparison with 'the proletariat of our times who hates and envies all' because he lacks any initiation or wisdom, before asserting that slavery has been imposed on the West with Roman culture, which he sees as a 'lunar, female, Semitic' conception without regard for heroism, beauty or individuality.

A little later, he states that after the murder of the Templar leaders and the destruction of the organization by Phillip IV of France, centuries of plague, famine and war would afflict Europe, culminating in the French Revolution, largely because no one was there to look after the interests of ordinary people.

According to him, European men were shorter in at least three centuries after the demise of the Templars because they were less well fed. The inability of the Catholic Church to properly look after its flock was driven by a massive internal conflict of identity arising from the Semitic concept of sin and original sin. This 'engraved blood and fire upon the world'.

So, we have seen that noble knights could work for spiritual goals and human welfare alike. In more modern terms, George Lucas touched peoples' consciousness when he portrayed a futuristic class of druid knights like the Templars, who protected worlds against the recurring darkness — the Jedi.

Spiritual knighthood is a sound and meritorious concept so why should we not establish, train and deploy such a force or devote considerable time to becoming members of such a force?

The second indispensable factor in fighting this necessary war against darkness is in bolstering the loyalty and cooperation of families — families and families of nations. All human leadership involves families so families are core elements in wider society and its leadership. Anavah has relevance then to all leaders, right down to fathers — the leaders of families. They must cultivate their powers of perception, be vigilant and be diligent.

In the ideal world, intervention would not be necessary and all nations would be ruled in peace and harmony but as things stand now in the war for the control of the world, leadership has been subverted both on a national and family level. Intervention will be necessary at both levels.

It might help to clarify the matter to think of the issue in the following terms. If a wife or child was being abused, they could not stop it themselves without outside assistance from the wider family or clan. Nations are like families or clans. When the people are being abused by their leaders, it is extremely difficult and dangerous for them to do anything about it themselves without outside assistance. When governments cross the line and become like abusive fathers, only other nations in the family of nations can judge them, censor them, restrict them and even dispose of them if necessary.

Consequently, to deal with the rapid spread of evil in the world today, the message must go out wide and a new organization of like minds from multiple member nations must be convened so that it can become the basis for the new more generous and compassionate nobility.

Such an organization must also have a clear, unequivocal code capable of guiding us through the complexities of a covert war, open war and a complex modern life. The concept of anavah teaches us that we must be perceptive, vigilant and diligent and that all sounds good — but about what?

It is all very well being vigilant in say, watching out for thieves but if you have no idea about con-men, what good will your vigilance do? Especially in our complex modern world, we need a comprehensive code that will help us systematically come to terms with all the relevant aspects of life in this, our existence.

Together, with such a code, a noble class in the various honourable nations would have a chance of fighting the dark shadow falling across our world but alone and without the code, even strong national groups would likely fail. Governments would suppress them and if they did not and a particular group succeeded in taking control of a country then other countries still dominated by the current criminal elements would invade and destroy them.

The change that is needed is something that can only be achieved if it is done internationally, involving strong groups from all of the member nations and by overcoming language barriers in the process.

Good leadership can only come from the heart. It has to be motivated and guided by a true sense of family, in which the leader or leaders care for their people as a good father would care for his wife and children — again integral with the concept of anavah, the essence of which will be explored later in greater detail.

In any case, the motives for such caring and effective leadership have a very complex and subtle foundation — one that cannot simply be taken on at the drop of a hat like a fur coat or a Macintosh.

Potential leaders with such deep foundations of care and responsibility are reared in families who exemplify that care in their internal workings. In our current degraded societies, such qualities at their best are rare. The foundations of leadership have to be solid but in most cases today, they are almost entirely absent.

In a new and carefully revised social structure, leaders would be chosen because they had such anavistic qualities but they would also be skilled in instilling such vital qualities into their children.

Executed with care and diligence, the growth and educational cycles in such families would improve with each successive generation, as would the skills in other families with more general roles.

Perhaps it is no mere coincidence that families are referred to intergenerationally as trees. When you bear in mind that trees have growth cycles that depend to a large degree on appropriate environmental conditions, you can begin to see the significance of the analogy. So, families can be seen as growing towards an ultimate purpose in the environment suited to them and the nature of that family should be seen as worthy of preservation.

Each family in the ideal society contributes to the ultimate developmental destiny of the individuals within it by guiding them consistently in the ways it knows most about. Degrading and de-structuring society, in part by providing individuals the absolute liberty to choose any occupation, does much to disrupt the social fabric and thereby inhibits the growth of happiness in society as a whole, not to mention the individual.

Looking at it from another point of view, if these modern freedoms to simply jump ship and abandon the occupations of our forefathers were so necessary and so important, surely they would create great happiness in people and in society generally?

Maybe these freedoms did create a certain amount of happiness in the beginning but with the way things work now, this supposed liberty ends up detracting far more from our lives than it's worth.

Our societies are already far too destabilised and the loss of a true sense of community alone cannot possibly be justified by choosing whether you grind a tooth or a piece of auto body or perhaps even the wit of some fellow lawyer.

The loss of true community in society is a major thing. It's like having to eat the meat without the gravy, like sex without love and like eating a piece of fruit that has no crispness or flavour. These deep-seated problems and our needs as gregarious social creatures must be fully understood before we can have any real chance of dealing with them.

So, is it really that bad to restrict (not ban) changing occupations between generations of families? Quality of life is more determined by how we do something than what we do, in any case.

Many children often willingly going on to follow in their parents' footsteps anyway. Any intelligent person will be able to see the advantages of family-based intergenerational upskilling and if people truly love what they do every day, they will usually engender a love for it in their children as well.

Where this occurs, it would be rare for the children not to enjoy the occupation their parents chose. In this case, society will be served well by increased stability and by an undisturbed trajectory of intergenerational upskilling courtesy of the intense and enduring sort of communication that family can enjoy.

The main drive towards children seeking different occupations to their parents is caused by a number of freak one-off social problems brought about through the current degraded condition of our society.

The first and most significant of these is the huge disparity of wages between different occupations. It contributes much to the envy and jealousy of which Miguel Serrano spoke. Doctors are paid more than drivers because there are more drivers than doctors and we need more doctors — but why do we need more doctors? Because our health system has become corrupted.

Certainly, being a doctor is more difficult than being a driver and I'm not suggesting that there should be no disparity in wages — simply not the sort of vast differences there are now. Also, being a doctor in a more constructive, benevolent society with a better run health system would be less difficult, less stressful and more spiritually rewarding.

The second problem leading to people wanting to choose an occupation different to their parents is the question of kudos. They simply want to earn more money and do something supposedly more important but truly, every job is important. It would not exist if it did not need to be done. Frequently, this quest for kudos happens because people are taught to value money over meaning and form over function.

Strangely, this same question of freedom has been brought to bear on our familial relationship choices as well in this stressful, unhappy degraded time in our history. Invidious elements imposing themselves on white cultures have been actively, persuasively encouraging mixed marriages through advertising, marketing, books, movies, games and a proliferation of not so subtle news media propaganda.

A mixed marriage may not necessarily be a bad thing on a personal selfish level but could there really be any net increase in the personal happiness it delivered sufficient to compensate for any costs that it might incur at other levels — possible familial conflict, possible losses of intelligence capacity, possible genetic incompatibilities, the gradual loss of racial integrity and the like?

Again, as with jobs, it is not so much about banning the practise but about not having it actively, aggressively encouraged by media and or government. After all, with race, who stands to gain from our already relatively small numerically white race mixing with other races? Not us, that's for sure.

Like every individual, family or race, we need strength. In a body, once full grown, change means corruption, aging, decay. Is it drawing too long a bow to say that change in the racial body by bringing in large amounts of foreign genes means the same thing?

Certainly, Rome began to fail when it started to allow all sorts of foreigners in as citizens.

Applying the same principle to job choice, youngsters should assume that they will follow in their parents' footsteps and if for some reason they really do not want to, they should be allowed to apply to seek a future in a field for which they have a great passion.

In a truly just society, it might actually be easier for them to do so, given the proper case being made for it, than under the current system.

Change does not have value simply for its own sake. Happiness and fulfilment are created in how people do things — not in what they do.

In our modern societies, around half of all people will experience severe and ongoing depression and along with the poor way that our work places are so often organized and run, this could be because people are not doing what is best suited to them.

Millions have died from drug overdoses. Millions more have suicided. Alcohol abuse destroys many more both in physical and psychological terms. Is this really better than life under the czars or the kings? In fact it is said that the Gnostics set up the Russian monarchy and church as a protection against evil and that while there was a Czar, evil could not flourish. The only religion they banned was Talmudic worship.

Ours is in fact a very unhappy society and I would not mind betting that a significant proportion of people fail to get any real fulfilment from their work.

So, having drawn that ugly picture, we now have good reason to consider the alternative. We can derive enormous benefit from re-introducing loyalty to a truly worthy hierarchy, to the family occupation and to our race. With this consistent loyalty, in time we will see valuable intergenerational upskilling and much more caring leadership that passes on its skills and sense of responsibility to successive generations.

Some might think it drastic and uncalled for to reintroduce a structured class system but if we exclude the least necessary and the least desirable aspects of it, would such a tiered class system look so bad?

Deep down, we all know who we are anyway, measured in part by what we are most comfortable doing in life, and if we are not made to feel bad about it by being abused, dishonoured and poorly recompensed, there should be no slight to our happiness.

In earlier centuries, people in the middle class hated those in the lowers classes and envied those in the upper class. These unproductive attitudes led to fruitless and even destructive conflict. People dwelt on and became obsessed by the notion of superiority. Yes, some people do have greater skills and intelligence but those who truly do will not see the need to harp on about it just as the gentle giant does not need to flex his muscles.

In a more intelligently run class-tiered society, perhaps a lot like the ones the Templars ran, the vast majority that makes up our working class would receive their due respect and live as comfortably as they do now in basic material things while many other material and spiritual things would be far superior because society, driven by greater spirit and expertise, would give more commitment to their creation.

Where the technology exists to create sufficient food and shelter for all and everyone's needs are met comfortably, the call of our forefathers to do what is in our hearts would satisfy us more than the prospect of accumulating vast moneys, which most cannot really attain now anyway.

Many retire from jobs as accountants or lawyers to grow a garden or to build wooden boats. Does this mean that they would have done that all along if they thought they could get by, living comfortably and owning their own home? In most cases, yes.

After having given up their culture and their freedom to push pencils for most of their lives, their financial freedom in retirement allows them to do what their heart truly desires.

Why did they ever need to push pencils then? The short answer is that the corrupt system of things wastes at least half of all money on the very administration of money; banking, insurance, accounting, cash handling, financial advice, investment and legal manoeuvres in overly complex legal frameworks.

This corrupt system of money and legalese is held in place by the very forces that enslave us and give us the pretend democracy of our current system.

So, why is our current leadership so bad? Why is it so greedy, hungry, uncaring and coercive? I could talk about all these but in particular, why is it uncaring?

I can only deal with this important question with reference to what I have experienced and heard. I know that many families operate without truly caring motives and in these families, it is virtually impossible to learn how to care for others.

My own family was not one of the worst I have seen or heard of but nor was it exactly ideal, and had I not been writing and researching solutions both in fiction and non-fiction forms, I might never have learned the true nature and value of care.

At worst, being reared in an uncaring family will teach people to exploit each other and treat each other as a commodity rather than as friends or loved ones. Such people will deal with others, given half the chance, like a conquered race or worse still like farm animals.

This is what our current politicians are — socially, emotionally retarded individuals who have sought the power to dominate people and exploit them. Only in representative democracy, with all its inherent weaknesses, could that happen.

So, what weaknesses does our representative democracy have? Yes, let us address that.

Firstly, the party system of preselecting candidates and demanding their absolute loyalty puts a gag over the mouths of good men and bad. The media then supports the illusion that there is an actual difference between the primary parties when it is generally no more than a juggling act between two rotten apples.

How these entities are run is partly a question of what people aspire to build but the attitude of leadership towards spirit and therefore the individual, is the largest determining factor in whether communal efforts will result in positive outcomes.

The goals of these organizations are currently short sighted. Their day-to-day administration reflects solely material concerns and their leaders fall over their feet in attempting to fulfil their perceived responsibilities to serve people. They are incompetent because they have no vision or sense of direction. They are the blind leading the — well, perhaps not so blind.

Allowing private funding in election campaigns cements this creaky system in place and is a sure sign of corruption. My brother, Mark, lives in the USA and one of his favourite popular sayings from American political culture is 'You got to dance with them what brung you,' also the name of a book on American politics by Molly Ivins. The popular saying reflects the fact that corruption is a big element in this political culture.

My father, Colin Mason, who was the deputy leader of a centre reformist party in the Australian Senate for nine years in the eighties, frequently had revealing stories to tell. One weekend, while visiting, he told me that he and his party colleagues had been offered substantial bribes to allow the foreign banks into the country.

'What sort of bribes?' I asked.

'Cash, in brown paper bags.'

'How much?'

'I couldn't say exactly,' he said, 'but it looked to me like many thousands.' (Many tens of thousands now.)

'Was this the first time?'

'For us, but not, I think, for the major parties.'

Colin was a stickler for honesty so I knew that it had happened and that it was apparently normal practise in the Australian Parliament. He did not accept the cash (nor did his party colleagues) and likely for that reason we have been targeted and held back as a family in many ways both large and small.

Interestingly, despite being Deputy Leader of the Australian Democrats for many years, when he passed in 2020 aged 93, not one mention was made of him in the legacy media.

Most heartless of all — a true stab in the back — the supposedly free and fair ABC completely ignored him and his life despite his having worked for them in several positions of great trust and responsibility for many years. This included establishing the ABC office in Singapore and holding the position as its chief there for a number of years then becoming deputy director of the ABC overall.

Later, he was given the great honour of overseeing the introduction of regional radio into Thailand. It was a massive job that required enormous heart and dedication, not only administering the technical aspects but coming up with a range of useful and imaginative programming to help the Thai people with the many difficulties they faced in their normal daily lives.

It is certain that the Thai people owe at least some small part of their current success today as an economic power to Colin's thoughtful and caring efforts in the introduction of this vital means of communications to large parts of Thailand.

When he returned to Australia in 1965 after around two years away, Colin resumed his work at the ABC and was assigned to create and produce strong current affairs programs for the newly introduced medium of television. In this leadership capacity, he was closely involved with some of the most important ABC TV current affairs programs of his time. All this, along with around fifteen books published worldwide and many hundreds of thousands of copies sold, was a huge achievement.

Yet he died without being remembered by the Australian people because of his affiliation with an honest centre party and very likely because he simply would not take bribes. That is how deeply corrupt Australia has become.

In numerous ways, Australia owed so much more to him, including the vast trade in raw materials with China that has made Australia so wealthy.

The first major trade between those two countries, a $25 million purchase of coal from Australia, ($250m now) was an offer made as a personal favour to my father by senior Chinese officials after he suggested a simple and cost-effective means for noise suppression in Chinese factories to prevent their workers going deaf.

On his account, he drew rough designs for simple noise baffles on paper napkins while at lunch with these officials while others on the Australian delegation simply talked and laughed amongst themselves.

Essentially, his care for Chinese workers and their conditions impressed the Chinese officials enormously and prompted them to begin what ultimately became a vast trade between our nations. Despite the many billions of dollars in profits it owes to him, the Australian establishment ignored the many remarkable achievements of his life.

This is just one argument as to why we need to abandon the old system of government in our western countries but it's the one that I know best, and I do not imagine for a minute that things are much different in other modern western nations.

Not so long ago, police in the UK were given the right to arrest people if they even had the suspicion of a protest meeting taking place. And recently, the French passed a law subjecting people to up to five years in prison merely for criticizing MRNA vaccines in any way.

The same forces that dishonoured my father have been set to work against us, eating away our lives, our honour, our happiness, our health and even our sense of power and responsibility.

Some people talk about life in terms of inevitable up and down cycles as if there was nothing we could do about it when we face downturn or decay.

Yet we can do great things and should think of things in more positive terms. To employ an off-roading analogy, it is like we are climbing a very difficult hill and beginning to lose traction near the top. If we fail to find some clever, innovative way at the right time to move onwards and upwards — a new technique to get traction or a means to find a little extra power — we might slip, turn sideways and roll over back down to the bottom receiving significant damage along the way.

Yet if we are clever and find a way to keep the wheels turning, we will arrive at the top, relax, admire the view and maybe even find a whole new country to explore.

Our lives are a voyage of sorts and to draw on another interesting comparison, democracy has never been found to work at sea. Too many dangers, too many uncertainties assail ships — therefore strong, inspired, unequivocal leadership is required. But are things really any safer or more certain in our lives on land?

No, after all it is still a voyage and it is still very difficult and dangerous, especially at the moment with governments all around the world funding dangerous bio-weapons research, including China now meddling with the deadly Nipah virus, and imposing unheard of biochemical coercion on people.

We would not want our lives to be the voyage of the damned so we need the qualities of anavah guiding us effectively on an intergenerational basis — enhanced perception, vigilance and diligence along with an unflinching willingness to learn.

Our current leadership is almost completely useless in large part because the system is useless and no wise or self-respecting man would subject himself to trying to lead under that system. A wise man knows that if you are going to do something then most of the time you would be better off not doing it at all than doing it badly.

Most of those listening to me or reading these words will have been frustrated in some way or other by the way things work in most of our modern societies. Fancy shmancy government funded protection bodies like the Australian 'Human Rights Commission' and the 'Anti-Discrimination Board' are really only paper cut-outs designed to look like they are protecting and serving the common man. In reality they do nothing of the sort.

Complex and expensive legal systems, adversarial government, oceans of red tape and an ignorant, biased media leave us with echo chambers and rules coming out of our ears that banish all delight and joy in life. In this rolling sea of fakery our elected representatives are deaf, dumb, blind and remote.

One of the principal weapons used against us in the current system of things is social division — the division of people by age, by gender, by language, by religion and by money, which leads to huge losses of understanding in individuals, families and societies, crippling every successive generation more completely.

We have all had enough and need positive direction facilitated by the clear comprehension of a truly just code rather than haphazard flip flopping, opportunism and low-level short-sighted expediency.

Leadership is a complex task that demands a great sense of duty and loyalty and those best suited to do it with creative, spiritual, innovative and adaptive minds should, over a number of generations, be promoted as a distinct class to rebuild the integrity and cultural strength of our societies.

In fact, this is the only way that such a thing could happen — by first building a guiding, leading class. No argument ever truly holds up against the idea that people can effectively change their lives by changing the way they think and this applies equally well to society as a whole because the best leadership comes from the inspiration of single minds.

Chapter 4 — The Spiritual Nature of Nobility

Instead of the tawdry and dishonourable reality we have been dealing with, we should expect better and consider just what would be needed in that new, better reality. If we were to work for a new system that put in place a genuinely noble class based in merit, what would those merits be?

The answer is quite simple. No extraordinary imagination is needed and to get us started, here is my initial take on it.

The Eight Requirements for Noble Leadership (8)

1. The responsibility to demonstrate genuine compassion for his fellow man.
2. Loyalty to family and nation manifesting right through to ensuring quality succession.
3. The honesty to respect the perception and the discovery of truth through intellectual rigor.
4. The diligence to learn constantly and find the right way.
5. The vigilance to perceive and foresee potential dangers.
6. Adherence to a comprehensive, coherent spiritual code.
7. Present well in a reassuring and unthreatening manner.
8. Love and trust life enough to be courageous in the face of adversity.

I know which of these some will dispute. Number seven might seem debatable and it could be argued that valuing presentation might lead to counter-productive physical discrimination but let's face it, this new class would accrue many advantages over time so the people in it would likely evolve towards fair appearance and graceful conduct in any case.

Also, the better conditions become in society in general, the more everyone else will become like that as well; less maimed, uncared-for and self-abandoned.

There is and always has been a natural impulse in us for trusting good appearance, which under our strange, perverted modern social system fails to achieve what nature meant for it.

Under more positive and natural conditions, where good appearance was allowed its natural influence subject to reasonable caveats, a positive force for good could be expressed.

Good looking, well-presented people are often a focus for attention and as such help to provide social cohesion. Given the proper understanding and respect for their natural role, such people would almost without exception respond with grace and consideration.

Nature has a use for almost everything and good appearance is no exception. If we follow nature here, the negative stereotypes can be weeded out from our culture and leave us with a great resource.

Deep down, we are all fascinated by charm and good looks and despite the fact that it might be no more than a basic natural drive, we can and often do build on basic natural drives very effectively. Better to build on them than to deny them.

Point number six addresses the need for a comprehensive spiritual code. Again, as in point eight, this is about trust. We need to trust that there is a reason for existence or we would not strive for excellence but if we listen to nihilist material dictates alone, no bell will sound. It is an important issue so I must stress that I will deal with the matter of spirit and the need for a sensible and binding spiritual code in more detail later.

Outside the above, few would even consider debating the validity of any of these prerequisites, except those of a distinctly communist persuasion and I'm sure as hell not likely to sway them in any case.

So, let's talk more about what defines nobility.

The foundation of nobility must be a commitment to hope and optimism and to finding the right way. Hope and optimism are clear concepts that few would dispute or not understand. They feed energy and commitment to achieving the most positive outcomes. Finding the right way might sound simple on the face of it but there are so many ways to choose from, so hope and optimism must have a part to play in guiding us.

From the language's many and complex roots, the right way is justice. That is what justice means. It means a system and or approach designed and geared towards finding the right way no matter how difficult that task is. Certainly, we could not abide a system of nobility or justice that allowed people like the fabled Sherriff of Nottingham free rein.

There would have to be systems for communicating disputes and appeal. There would have to be a bill or schedule of human rights, which interestingly in this political covid crazy time, my home country of Australia does not have nor has ever had.

Debate in the noble house, whatever it would be called, would centre around issues raised by nobles or by the king and would be subject to clear guidelines of logic and reason. Members would be asked to vote for or against each proposal and groups based on these votes would consult in temporary alliances to discover and present the best possible cases.

The king would hear and comment on each case made then decide the matter after all the issues had been teased out. He would always be obliged to provide his reasoning and the case presenters would be required to comment on the quality of the reasoning.

Emotion could be a valid determinant of the king's choice in rare circumstances but if used would have to be clearly stated and acknowledged as such. There would be no set points-based system upon which the king would make his final judgement but he would need to be aware of the need to listen both to reason and emotion. He would also have to weigh the statements of the informed nobles and make a clear case against them if he disagreed.

If he made a decision where emotion was a major consideration, he would have to explain why. Such an emotion-oriented decision would be immune to challenge only for certain very specific reasons, such as when insufficient data was available with which to properly make a reasoned choice and a choice had to be made straight away.

The king's decisions would have to be ratified by adherence to stated goals and logic, and the goals would have to be in accord with the binding code. Where the king decided against the will of the nobles, the decision could later be tabled amongst others, if the decision led to substantial loss of a significant kind, as cause to dethrone the king.

Carefully considered basic rules of logic would be the determining factors in debate rather than force of will or sheer weight of numbers.

If the king flouted the rules, his peers would be entitled to set a date for a hearing to remove him. A certain, relatively small minimum number of major errors would be needed to trigger investigation — perhaps three.

Under such extreme circumstances, a new king might have to be chosen. Given the need for numerous quality candidates, the above system might not work as envisaged in the early days of the monarchy until there was a ready supply of regal heirs to choose from in replacing him.

If a king, in the long-term system, could be undermined and simply replaced by a powerful noble on whim, the system could not work. There might be some volatility in the early days of such a system but in the long term there would have to be a complex system of leadership succession in which numerous sons who were potential able monarchs were available to contest.

In a well-balanced system, removal of the king would be seen as futile and irresponsible unless he clearly breached the encoded philosophy of rule but if perchance such a man disgraced the office, there would need to be ample contenders to replace him. Each would then have to contend with others of the nobility until such time as sons of sufficient age and quality were ready to prove their worth and viability according to the same philosophy of rule.

Also, if there was sufficient love for the monarch and his family, a regent could be chosen by the same means until a son or sons were ready to contend.

So, having briefly covered the matter of the future monarch, we should return to the nobility. There would be a considerable burden of responsibility on nobles so, with a strong code of leadership in place, it would seem pertinent to ask, who would want such a job unless they were well-suited for it?

Those without hope or the vision of a better world would simply not bother to apply or would be weeded out if they did. The lack of a vision of a better world would tend to indicate a lack of positive energy and might lead to corruption either by self or by others. Moreover, those without hope find it easier to be expedient and to allow injustice.

Few now espouse noble values or sentiments in large part because nobility currently seems like a lost cause. Yet those who hold to such a vision loyally in these most adverse of conditions would likely demonstrate the required spiritual purity and insight needed for holding such an office.

In some ways, holding loyalty to the ideal of building the best possible world requires considerable sacrifice. If a person was to maintain the right sort of mind-set, they could not allow themselves to take short-cuts and could not avert their eyes from the guiding light of the truth. Many attractive offers might have to be passed up by such men. Many advantages might need to be foregone. So, why would you seek to serve when such service asks such weighty sacrifice?

The answer is that the decision can only have reference to the inner life of the person. The inner being, the spiritual code and the long-term vision are the only things that truly have enduring value and this is very clear to a genuinely noble mind.

In our modern world of social and personal corruption through sabotaged culture, people have flawed views about noble qualities so it might help to explore the meaning of anavah in encompassing what it means to be a true noble.

The most obvious noble quality that springs to mind is a sense of noblesse oblige, a quality which draws most directly on the single element of diligence. The current commonly held view of this would have the nobility serve the people without hope of decent reward or compensation or even that they should sacrifice themselves life and limb to the group.

Such a notion is nonsense. What sane person would ever do such a thing and why should they? If the group structure requires blind sacrifice it has already failed and should be immediately replaced.

Never sacrifice your life for lies or boring, stupid irrelevancies but under very rare circumstances, in times of great need, you might choose to achieve something great especially if loss of life or limb was likely to eventuate anyway.

No, your service should not be to some flawed concept of social unity but rather to building and to diligently holding true to a guiding set of spiritual principles.

Social unity is not a forefront goal to be achieved at all costs but simply a manifestation of right behaviour, just as a clear head and a light heart is a reflection of hard and worthy work.

If we are to free ourselves from the burdens of fear, division and exploitation we must have a clear life code suitable for the modern world and this code must draw on the absolute, unmitigated need for acute perception, diligence and vigilance — the key elements of the concept of anavah.

If such a code was to be set in place and adhered to effectively, it would need a cast iron, well-bred class of people to administer it. The diligence of these people would have to be geared towards adherence to the principles rather than towards any specific sacrifice of their time or of their person.

Such people might not be wealthy or influential under the current system but under a better one their personal qualities would allow them to generate great wealth, to hold it gracefully and to use it wisely.

People in general should not aspire to great wealth and power unless they have a clear visionary need for it. The cost to the natural world of a great many wealthy people is too great and many wonderful things in life, after all, do not require great wealth to allow us to experience them.

A modest set of aspirations is undoubtedly a good thing for most people, especially because of how it will affect the natural world yet simply because a person has little means does not signify that they should be scorned or half-starved or deprived of social, emotional and intellectual status or interaction.

There are many ways in which people can improve their lives without high income or dangerously negative environmental effects and given how important this is, it is interesting to note that the majority of skills needed for spiritual and social development are not significantly harder to obtain than those needed to meet the basic material challenges of life.

Given that I do not advocate wealth equality in this future system, the concept of wealth should be well-discussed. Not everyone can be rich in terms of great wealth and luxuries. Resources clearly limit the numbers of those who can be — so the relevant question here is whether there should be any wealthy people at all.

For one reason or another we are very ambivalent about wealth. Most of us despise it as much as we desire it and this confusion might well be part of the social and moral sabotage that has been inflicted on us.

Part of the reason why we desire wealth so much is because so many details of recorded history and many instances of our own experience tell us that we will suffer terribly and perhaps even be deprived of our own lives if we fail to secure substantial wealth.

And a big part of why we despise it is clearly because so much ill has been done with it. Yet, under the right system we would not need to worry about either of these negative facets of wealth.

With reasonable efforts we could obtain everything we needed both for survival and for fulfilment and with the right people in possession of great wealth under the guidance of a code primarily espousing perception, vigilance and diligence, wealth would do as it should.

Yes, so an effective noble class should be seriously wealthy for a number of very good reasons, and I will further elaborate on these reasons now.

Firstly, they would own great estates and owning them would take great pride in their proper management and efficiency. At least within these estates they would readily be able to make the most of their wealth to give the most shared benefit to their people. Yet conducting these estates would also give them experience and insights that they could effectively apply when considering the wider needs of the nation.

Secondly, many great human exploits can only be initiated when there are people of great wealth to support them and get them under way. If the funds required for such projects were not owned by nobles but were public funds instead, those in control of them would choose less carefully and administer them less assiduously. That is why funds spent by public servants and employees of large corporations are spent so wastefully. Bureaucracy is the single worst element of our current political system and ironically, this is also what is wrong with our current capitalist system.

Thirdly, an honest political system should also be very clear and open about what it awards to its powerful citizens without any deception or excuse, for all to see. Where funds are not provided to assist with the great burden of responsibility on such people, they might pursue less worthy or honest sources of income.

Men in such positions would certainly have the greatest need for substantial wealth for the full and proper administration of their duties and if these funds were awarded openly and responsibly, it would inspire trust in and loyalty to the system.

So, we return to the matter of the spiritual nature of nobility and the new spiritual code that all levels of society could and should aspire to.

As an experienced fiction writer, I have considered questions of this sort in great depth. It can be argued that the processes of creating quality fiction reward writers with a unique capacity to place themselves deeply into situations that can reveal good solutions.

Writers consider varied sets of life conditions more frequently and more completely than anyone else. They build whole panoramas of life for multiple characters and must maintain a clear overview of how everything works. They are also deeply absorbed by the problems facing their characters and are motivated to better encompass the range of solutions to those problems.

Incidentally, absorption of new ideas also comes more easily to readers when they are engrossed in fiction, making the reading of fiction an indispensable means of facilitating learning and imparting knowledge, a tradition that has been passed down from generation to generation through the ages from time immemorial.

For example, my most recent fiction writing obliged me to create an integrated and coherent social code that eventually led to the discovery of the core seven-point canon that should govern and guide all human interaction — a specific element of my envisioned code that would be an utterly indispensable life reference.

Regard, curiosity, communication, trust, honour, vigilance and courage are the vital successive elements of this seven-point canon, broadly reflecting the seven key human estates — farming, building, politics, media, justice, public service and the military although each are also present in every individual's life.

Each quality can be seen to lead reliably to the next but the greater detail of the process of how they interact will be revealed later.

The Code of Mindcraft and the Spruce Arcana

Suffice it to say for the moment that the overall code of 'Mindcraft' created in my fiction series Reign of the Dragon serves practical goals, both material and spiritual, that are absolutely crucial to creating greater human happiness.

Anavah tells us to be vigilant but if we are to be, we must know the broad basic range of things about which we must seek to be perceptive and vigilant.

This vital core of Mindcraft is **The Spruce Arcana**. A tree is the best metaphor for the underlying requirements of strength, beauty and growth so the best sort of tree to represent the idea needs to be tall, supple and strong. A pyramidal shape is appropriate for reasons that I will shortly reveal. Hence, the spruce tree fit the picture admirably.

The key spheres and qualities of existence about which we need to be perceptive, vigilant and diligent are represented by the numbers 1 through 9 from top to bottom of the tree.

1   The singularity of the spiritual source
2   The duality of material existence
3   The three phases of intellectual discovery
4   The four planes of manifest existence
5   The five elements of nature

6   The six fundamental emotions
7   The seven-point canon of social interaction
8   The eight essential attributes of leadership
9   The nine great desires

Our comprehension of this world best starts with the power of the singularity, which many people believe is the source of all creation. That is represented by the number 1 at the top of the tree.

Our material reality is defined most fundamentally by the concept of duality, represented by the number 2, and when we understand it, we understand the rest.

The way we engage with this reality is by discovering and learning, and this process has three basic stages — assumption, doubt and resolution represented by the number 3.

As learning opens up we can see that we need to define and appreciate the four different planes of interaction of which we are aware in this existence — the material, the physical, the astral / emotional and the causal / conceptual. They are represented by 4.

In pagan times, we saw the world in terms of the four basic elements plus the ether or the intangible and this set of elemental definitions helps us understand the way we interact with the physical and material world. This is represented by 5.

We understand the intellectual in terms of our basic process of discovery in 3 but we must also define and include the emotional to balance this. The core emotions number 6, which I will specify later.

With a good emotional-intellectual balance we can build the best sort of social interaction and the already mentioned basic canon of social interaction so vital to leading life well in this world includes elements numbering 7.

The set of definitions of required positive leadership attributes mentioned earlier number 8.

The core group of fundamental desires that drive us in our journey through this world, and which reveal much about our own nature, specified later, number 9.

If we were to have a dedicated, honourable and truly noble class administering a code such as this and living it with steadfast commitment to finding the right way, our world could become a virtual paradise.

Chapter 5 — What the New World Would Look Like

It is all very well to propose some abstract ideal of a new system that will provide all the answers but the fact is none of it would be possible without a vision — a vision of just what the world could look like. In this, the first principle of anavah, enhanced perception or 'having the eyes to see, is indispensable.

In this world, young Brad would wake up early and jump out of bed and run in to greet his parents with a broad grin because the day's promise would beckon him like a moth to a candle. His days are filled with love, exploration, communication, creativity and sport. He has respect and regard both from his teachers and his peers. The process of learning is an adventure of excited discovery rather than the drudgery of rote learning a bunch of irrelevant 'facts'.

Dominic, his father, will happily spend this day in the fields because the weather's fair and beautiful and many others like him will share that work so necessary to all. Heavy rain is predicted for several days in two days time and work in the snug, well laid out machine shop will wait until then.

Katie will spend the day at the creche with the twins and for an hour or two in the afternoon Dom will join her there with other fathers to help build some fun new play equipment and tend to the heavier jobs in the garden. The twins will lend a hand with her duties under her careful guidance.

At the end of the week, the local earl and his party will come to attend the ritual cleansing in the sparkling river and take seat afterwards at the great table in the town keep. He owns and loves every square inch of the land of this county and keeps a careful eye on it.

With a dozen such towns under his care in the county, he attends each of them for such ceremonies at least once a year. He will compliment Katie's blueberry tarts on their rich flavour and will ask his wife to engage her services for the king's visit later that year. Dom will speak to him on the matter of the growing demand for his excellent farm machinery and ask for the allocation of more space and two new apprentices, made possible by the near completion of the town housing construction program.

At the meeting, the townspeople will be shocked to learn that someone in the next county came down with a cold, something unheard of in twenty years.

Well, I could go on and write a full novel about it but my point by now is clear. Life does not need to be painful, degrading and hopeless. Nor does it need to be full of gadgets, trinkets and bulging bank accounts. It can be simple yet busy, exciting and fulfilling.

Young Brad would get more real excitement from watching his father demonstrate his new worm-friendly earth tilling machine to the earl than some current day freak enjoying a jet ski ride under the influence of a heady mix of weed and speed.

We really do not need all that rubbish. What we do need is regard, curiosity, communication, trust, honour, vigilance and courage.

We do not need to be sacrificing ourselves for the mythical group for no real gain. That is the ideology of communism and invariably the only people such sacrifice benefits are the unscrupulous leaders of the group. Then we get 'great revered leaders' like Kim Jong Un who watch their people starve while they live in luxury.

In fact, a new society ruled by a monarch and nobles need not be cruel, unfair, unjust or dishonourable, as we saw with the Templars. People would be happier and healthier in properly run feudal communities.

Most monarchies in the past worked very well for many hundreds of years, as demonstrated by a number of notable monarchs including Phillip II of Austria, Alfred the Great of England and Charlemagne of the Franks (son of Charles Martel who beat off the Moslems and forged the first European empire) but even they were not set up properly from the outset with a carefully worked out plan and a comprehensive code of behaviour.

The new Empire of the Ever-Rising Sun would be a true family, a wider family, yes, with a hierarchy but with a hierarchy that reflected familial principles.

Does a good father starve his children of decent food, beat them mercilessly, submit them to experimental medications of no long-term value, allow them to fall victim to an array of unnecessary dangers, dress them in toxic plastic clothing and imprison them in cages when they object?

The fact is, we are seeing these evil sorts of manifestations now in our supposed democracy and the reason we are seeing them is because no one man takes ultimate responsibility in this fake system, as a father would with his family.

In the new empire, the monarch would be presented with issues for debate in parliament or would raise them himself. He would offer solutions and his nobles would consider the pros and cons. Debate would ensue until the issue was resolved.

If the monarch could not accept the consensus of his peers, he would have to state the reasons why he could not. Sometimes, after all, intuition trumps reason for we do not always have access to all the facts and under these circumstances, he would say that he had doubts about the completeness of the information.

At this point, he would appoint three nobles to investigate the matter, appoint associates from relevant classes to increase their insight, consult specialists and come back with more detailed information, whereupon a decision would be made from their determinations. Yet in the end, the king would carefully check and peruse their findings and have the final say.

According to the spiritual code that would be governing the nobles and the king, every decision would be open to change depending on the emergence of new factors. Some matters require decisions and actions that once implemented cannot easily be revised or changed. Any such decision made that proved in error would be logged as a significant precedent to be examined and discussed in greater detail.

If the king made a decision with which less than a third agreed and it turned out to be wrong, this would be logged against his record. Three such instances might invoke contest, which would require the king to stand for reselection amongst a range of candidates qualified for contest at that time. Strict and inviolable rules would govern whether any potential candidate was qualified to take part in the contest. Punishment could not be easily instituted against a dethroned monarch but he would be reduced to the lowest level of nobility.

Leadership would change for no other reason and all going well, the king's leadership would pass on to an heir of his own blood; an heir who would have stood in strong contest for leadership with all the other qualifying king's heirs. The choice would not necessarily be the eldest, the wealthiest or the physically strongest but the one who met the carefully defined criteria for excellent leadership most closely. Every successive king would be chosen from the qualifying heirs in such a way.

Ideally, the process could be started by the monarch before his death to clarify succession, especially if his qualifying children had all reached the age where they could contend. Allowing the greatest number of heirs to contend that is possible would do much to ensure the succession of the best possible monarch.

The broader society would be defined in part with reference to the core concept of anavah, in part by the more detailed spiritual code and in part by a constitution that defined both general human rights and specific citizen rights.

The constitution would specify such things as the right to enjoy just freedoms in doing what you are born to do in the way you wish to without hurting anyone, to be treated fairly, to be free not to be forced into any act impinging on personal freedom, to be happy and healthy and to keep the larger part of the fruits of your labours.

The one exception to this substantial set of freedoms would involve work occupation. Every social mechanism would attempt to preserve the traditional occupations of families but the constitution would specify a person's right to petition parliament for a change of occupation which would be allowed if the reasons outweighed the merits of intergenerational family upskilling.

Such a thing might occur if a man's father died before his son could properly gain the skills of his life occupation or if the son could cite cogent reasons why that occupation was unsuitable to him. Further weight would be added to the case if he could arrange to train under a suitable mentor in his chosen new occupation.

In most significant instances the nobles and the monarch would be the law but in more trifling day to day legal matters there would be minor judges and advocates. There would of course need to be a legal system. That system would differ from ours most significantly in that there would be no 'letter of the law' in the sense of there being endless detailed roadblocking regulations.

Precedents could be cited but they would only be contributory elements rather than determining ones. Every case is different and while precedents might weigh in the determination of justice, they could not be the sole determinants. Therefore, the clear spirit of the law and the individual factors in the case would determine right and wrong. Accumulating regulations and specifications in the law lead eventually to unworkable complexity and a corrupt legal system.

The fundamental concepts that would govern the spirit of the law in this new society are specified below.

The New Social Law Model from the Code Wars

Premise:
There is an individual and a society of individuals and every society should aim to facilitate the individuals' journeys through intellectual and emotional understanding towards the higher state of spiritual awareness.

The group is there to serve the individual in a balanced way to provide physical and material security that furthers the individual's understanding of the relationship between the temporal and the spiritual.

On this journey, both the individual and the society must be aware of and explore the concept that careful thought and control of the mind are the primary sources of personal power and fulfilment.

This would include the idea that consciousness is increased when careful thought is used to reveal structure and meaning, and when control of the mind brings clearer perspective.

Higher knowledge encompasses both the manifestation of structure and meaning and the awareness of it, therefore enabling the mind, through careful thought, to rule over matter.

Chapter 6 — So, What is Spirit?

It might seem superfluous to discuss what spirit is. Some will believe it exists and others will not but if we discuss it comprehensively, there will be less doubt and doubt can be both dangerous and destructive.

A well-known scientist once said: 'the field is the sole governing agency of the particle'. This could also be used as an analogy for how intangible energy is the sole governing agency of the physical world. The collective function of the mind, defined as 'spirit' by some, and at the very least driven by spirit, could be viewed in exactly those terms — what governs the physical world.

Few of us are adequately aware of spirit given that it has become fashionable to divorce ourselves from belief in such things. It has certainly become popular amongst scientists to propose that there is no spirit or inner being of any kind. The awareness of self is, according to some of them, only an illusion — no more than an inner image supported by psychobiology — hormones, neurotransmitters and the like.

Yet there is clearly more. This chapter is fairly long but if we are to reach a good understanding of just how big a part spirit plays in our lives, we need to look at each the following aspects:

Spirit in the Here and Now
Spirit and Consciousness
Spirit and Identity
Spirit and Emotions
Spirit and Big Picture Goals
Spirit and the Stigma of Religion
Spirit and Life
Spirit and the Arcane Mysterious
Spirit and Energy Within (1)
Spirit and the Afterlife

A Natural Metaphor to Summarize Spirit
Spirit and Navigating Life in this World
Spirit and Faith

Spirit in the Here and Now

There is no doubt that the issue must be faced. Is the human spirit enduring and real or is it as ephemeral as a mist that burns off in the sun? Well, even if spirit is a result of chemistry and does not outlast the purely physical life chemistry, it can still be demonstrated that it exists just as much as any physical thing. After all, the physical, as opposed to the material, also disappears in functional terms upon death.

So, let us address this issue. Is spirit an illusion any more than the physical which is after all only temporary? Also, it is very easy to claim that something non-material is an illusion yet there are many non-material things we accept every day as reality.

So, we need to ask ourselves what is real but is not material or physical and of course there are plenty such things. All sorts of emotions clearly qualify both as real and as elements of spirit. So too do human endeavours — creativity, invention and even exploration. Spirit drives all these very real things and is effectively expressed in them as well.

Fortunately, life does offer up clues to careful observers that it does consist of something more than mere physical or material substance. Many people have powerful spiritual experiences during their lives and the marvellously coherent, beautiful and meaningful patterns of the world are in alignment with the purposeful nature of our coherent individual thought.

Where the highest material ambition possible for human science is indisputably to enhance the accessible fund of knowledge and thinking about nature, in other words to collect coherent meaning, it is reasonable to conclude that the purposeful patterns observed in nature express meaning and hint at higher meaning — a higher meaning that can be defined as a code.

Adding weight to this reasonable conjecture about the existence of higher meaning is the incontrovertible truth that no one can truly say what does not exist before they know all that does. After all, does an infant know about electricity or jet engines or political theory?

Spirit and Consciousness

It is vitally important that we resolve this issue of spirit because acceptance or rejection of it directly affects our state of consciousness. The human race is becoming a sad and incompetent lot with a limited outlook for the future and this may be, at least in part, because of an escalating acceptance of the view that existence is ultimately pointless.

So, on what premise is such a view founded? Is it because we have clearly proved there is nothing more than cogs and wheels? Is it because there would be some actual advantage in determining that?

No, we have not and no there would be no advantage in it because it is simply not possible to do so and the only advantage there could possibly be in trying to prove it, would be to be able to say that nobody was pulling the wool over your eyes — that you're nobody's fool. This is always the driving aim of the habitual sceptic — I only believe in facts. Well, my friends, that is actually the philosophy of the cave man — the cave man that did not invent the lever or the bucket or the wheel. "I do not believe in anything greater than I can see," defines an abysmal ignorance.

So why else would anyone prefer to believe that we are nothing more than cogs and wheels? What could be the rationale? What purpose would it serve? Is it possible that this scepticism holds sway in many simply because they do not dare hope that there is any more to life?

If so, it is both perverse and circular and really qualifies as nothing more than simple despair — a negative conscious state characterized by the loss of the ability to hope.

Why then, do people despair?

Spirit and Identity

The simple answer to that question is that without long-term security of identity, there can be no stable platform from which to express self, particularly in making good, reliable, constructive choices. Without good, reliable, constructive choices, chaos rules and ails the spirit. Too much chaos breeds insecurity and reinforces a flawed sense of identity.

This is clearly a vicious circle founded on the fundamental identity insecurity of spiritless nihilism and leads to escalating despair on the wider, social scale — but it is important to note that it happens in individuals first. In all this, individual identity is the little understood and central concept.

Sceptics say that people will never be anything other than physical beings but there are good reasons to consider more compelling alternatives.

Before accepting the spirit-crushing idea that we are condemned to exist for the whole of our lives solely in a state of blind materialism, not to mention accepting the dull prospect of permanent dissolution when our bodies fail, at least a little energy should be expended on looking somewhat deeper into the matter — deeper, I hope, than in any blind belief stemming from that creaking materialistic anachronism, 'the church' or indeed any of the JCI organized religions.

Firstly, as mentioned before, are there any non-material things of value that people already have —

things that are real, that express spirit and as such contribute to identity? Of course there are. There are all those things previously mentioned and many more but in the interests of brevity I'll offer just a few more examples.

There is the power of language itself through which we express all sorts of things driven by spirit. Then there is the delight of figuring out how something works, the excitement of discovering something new, the pleasure of hearing or creating a great piece of music or a beautifully expressed poem, all of which excite our spirits and contribute a great deal to making our lives worth living.

Careful and considered conversation, perhaps over a fine dinner, is a valuable expression of spirit. Love, loyalty and compassion cannot be lightly dismissed as matters of spirit. Then there are those moments when you think nobody cares about you but just at the right time, someone comes along and offers something loving and thoughtful. That is the highest testimony to spirit and will lift your spirits.

These are all real yet intangible, non-physical, non-material elements of enhanced consciousness that come from spirit, have an effect on our spirits and contribute much to our sense of identity. They are all acts of life; careful conscious perception and self-expression that also express the great and glorious supremacy of mind over matter — and without doubt, they are real for those who have the eyes to see.

All of these would not exist but for someone's conscious choice that they should and that they will. It really is as simple as that.

It cannot be denied that these things come from a sense of and capacity of spirit and contribute to its expression in the manifest world but how does it contribute, if it all, to our identity?

Identity is tied up closely with consciousness and in the west, this issue has been so poorly explored that most western people would describe their understanding of it in terms of Freud's exploration of the unconscious. It is known best then, perhaps, by what it is not.

In the east, however, various breeds of spiritual guides have defined conscious identity as 'the observer' behind the focusing prism of the human intellect and the emotions. So, if this observer is consciousness and it can draw on spirit, as we know it can, to express matters of spirit, surely acknowledging it will enable us to experience it all the more fully?

If we learn to reinforce this quality so crucial to creating positive emotions, will we not experience positive emotions all the more consistently? Then is this not a question of building and reinforcing identity through positive feedback?

So, by comparison, if we ignore spirit and do not cultivate an awareness of it, will we not suffer negative emotional consequences and run the risk of experiencing identity based solely on our direct experiences, all too often negative, of the world?

In this sense, if we are aware of spirit, are we not taking control of our experience and interaction with the world rather than letting it dictate the terms of how we feel and respond to it? The popular song, 'Always Take the Weather with You' expresses this admirably.

In short, I do believe that believing in the most positive thing about our metaphysical situation will result in our having a better experience of life.

Spirit and Emotions

A constructive view of spirituality that boosts positive emotions is certainly possible. Whether or not you choose to accept a belief in the metaphysical, ethereal existence of spirit, the search for a better life and more coherent identity must include a clearer understanding of the spiritual significance of the relationship between intellect and emotions, which for most people nowadays means developing their emotional intelligence.

So, what are the potential gains of this form of spiritual understanding?

Someone seeking a more enhanced consciousness through understanding their emotional selves more fully would hope to experience a heightened or maximized state of awareness, wherein perceptions were clearer, brighter and more delightful. Their intellectual brain function would also be more acute and the sense of self more lucid and coherent.

These sorts of gains are broadly sought in some sorts of religious asceticism although the yogi adepts, for instance, seem to take a very roundabout sort of route in attempting to achieve it — an approach that seems to deny the value of positive emotions and desires.

Compared to Richard Bach's path in his delightful classic 'Jonathan Livingstone Seagull', the yogis are painfully long-winded and prone to misguidance.

To cut through the bullshit, the simple fact is that the human mind can be more awake or less so, both emotionally and intellectually. People go through cycles of varying states of consciousness every day, between sleeping and waking whether or not they are in fact awake or asleep.

Acknowledging this, we regularly employ various means to enhance consciousness at least temporarily. Some use coffee, cocaine or even LSD but the yogis were right about one thing. Chemical shortcuts to enhanced coherency (emotional and intellectual) of identity are unreliable. You can only go so far with them and then the desired progress falters.

In sharp contrast to this, there are a range of effective mental discipline techniques that bring greater focus to consciousness. These techniques are generally based on verbal clarity (written, spoken or thought) and mental discipline conducive to positive attitudes. They create emotional muscles that do much to foster positive reinforcement and thereby allow the individual to keep on raising the spiritual potential.

Given that our consciousness is most influenced by the state of interaction between the two primary mind elements of intellect and emotions, it seems likely that the goal of enhancing consciousness would be facilitated not only by applying discipline to intellect but also by cultivating a full emotional life. To do this, intellect needs to be guided towards sorting out and reinforcing the potential of emotions.

Avoiding emotions will not allow you to learn how to understand and deal with them and appreciation is the whole point — appreciation by the observer within.

By enhancing intellectual function, the 'observer' has the potential to assess the world more reliably through the filter of the intellect, rather than solely through the raw perceptual capacity of the senses and the basest forms of emotions, thereby increasing spiritual balance and promoting lucid awareness. In effect, intellect can be used to enhance emotions and positively integrate itself with them.

The observer appreciates both physical senses and feelings then with greater clarity and becomes more able to analyse how to react to them to continue enhancing consciousness — the awareness and expression of spirit. In the wake of this process, if an individual attains the proper balance, the two vital primary aspects of mind will work smoothly in concert with each other.

The goal of maximized consciousness can only be achieved if both mental polarities, intellectual and emotional, function alongside each other with smooth efficiency. If they are fragmented instead, perception will be muddied and obscured, analysis will be flawed and expression will be incoherent. That would inhibit both the perception and the expression of spirit and would lead to a more negative emotional experience.

Spirit and Big Picture Goals

Any sane person would wish to make their life experience more lucid and colourful yet this is not achievable by direct or material means. There is a bigger, longer term picture to see. Whether you are currently desperately miserable or comfortably complacent, any deficit of conscious awareness will eventually manifest in your expressing destructive behavioural tendencies that bring on inevitable negative consequences.

On the other hand, choosing to overcome mental torpidity and live more consciously on a lasting basis will lead to both constructive spiritual effects and positive material outcomes.

There are many ways in which people can improve their lives without high income or dangerously negative environmental effects and given how important this is, it is interesting to note that the majority of skills needed for spiritual and social development are not significantly harder to obtain than those needed to meet the basic material challenges of life.

Considering the economy of effort that can be had in achieving both sorts of goals at once, it is strange that so little has been done to synchronize them.

Spirit and the Stigma of Religion

Given the easily achievable fringe benefits, there are many good reasons to consider the implications of there being such a thing as spirit. Yet despite the obvious benefits of cultivating spiritual qualities of harmony and intellectual fulfilment, a huge number of people strive solely for material success without any thought of gaining spiritual awareness along the way.

Given that spiritual values can be cultivated along the way, at no great cost, this seems to indicate the presence of subconscious resistance to doing so.

Yes, spirituality can hold a stigma for some, as I have already mentioned, depending on their attitudes. For these people, it might be like Tai Chi in the park. They would worry too much about what others think and would never contemplate going and waving their arms around in public on a Sunday morning.

Yet true spirituality is not what most people seem to think it is.

Yes, in general it has come to be associated with softer, clingier and more compassionate behavioural standards. Maybe such compassion has come to be seen as silly and weak through its association with so many absurd mainstream religious beliefs.

Well, if you do not mind throwing the baby out with the dirty water, so be it — but in this case, the baby is crucially important. The fact is, there is a huge difference between the spiritual and the religious. Many of the worst charlatans are religious without being the least bit spiritual so why not applaud the spiritual that is not the least but religious?

A negative attitude towards spirituality has spilled over from the dirty pot of religion over time and infects the cultural arenas of politics, bureaucracy, the police, business, unions and workplaces while the ludicrous BS of religious authority and doctrine survives with utterly undeserved respectability as a sort of fossilized icon of propriety and conventionality.

Given this, it is crucial to understand how patterns of social conformity tending towards the unthinking rejection of kind and compassionate behaviour are ultimately self-defeating.

In societies blighted by murder, rape, suicide and accident trauma, it can only accelerate harm to shun and discourage kindness. Wander too far down that road and you've got the horrific 'reevers' from Jos Whedon's cult movie 'Serenity'.

Spirituality might be seen by the undiscriminating as a kooky offshoot of religion but a 'no bull' assessment reveals it as simply the disciplined and consistent evaluation and modification of the state of one's consciousness.

Spirit and Life
Many believe that there is a spirit in some form or other, although most tend only to see it in terms of hopeful beliefs about life after death.

Spirituality can, however, be something more basic, real and alive, and if seen instead in terms of positive adjustments of personal attitudes and feelings affecting the enthusiasm with which life is embraced, it has a more immediate relevance.

Think of words like conviviality, vitality, invitation. They all come from the French word for live and when the French use this word, they mean spirit.

With the right spirit, life goes right in surprising ways both exciting and down-to-earth. When we mount spirited defences to attacks made upon our freedom, we practise the way of anavah and are touched by god in the way he intended. When we sing with spirit, the day becomes brighter. When a pony seems spirited, is it simply about him dashing around randomly?

No, we might assume such banality if we were in an ignorant frame of mind but really, it's because he's trying to communicate something vitally important to all who can see; the reality of energy and enthusiasm — in fact a great joy in and sense of wonder for life.

Exploring beyond the tangible in this way can be materially rewarding as well but it would be a waste to motivate oneself in such exploration with the fringe benefits alone. The benefits to mood and spirit are far more important than any material benefits that might come along with a spirited response to life.

In the absence of spirit, having it all can seem surprisingly empty, not to mention temporary, whereas spending a little time on discovering the spiritual secrets of inner awareness can lead to an enduring sense of 'having it all' in a way that nothing else can.

Spirit and the Arcane Mysterious

Some might see this state of self-knowledge as elevated consciousness while others call it spiritual liberation but either way it can lead to experiences far more rewarding than most would set out to hope for. The mysterious, the arcane and the exciting unknown add so much to life that when they are maximised, much can be added to the enduring sense of self.

Given a willingness to explore all avenues in the process, the truly intriguing manifestations of personal spirituality can be liberated and proceed from life as surely and naturally as day follows night.

The power of dreams, the astonishing freedom of astral projection, telepathy, creative insight and social positive emotion projection are all very real aspects of the arcane knowledge that we can and do tap.

The basic elements you need on the path to this spiritual awareness of our wider existence can be seen in Mindcraft's nine-point Spruce Arcana, the fundamentals of which are as follows working down from the top of the mystic tree.

1 The singularity of the spiritual source
2 The duality of material existence
3 The three phases of intellectual discovery
4 The four planes of manifest existence
5 The five elements of nature
6 The six fundamental emotions
7 The seven-point canon of social interaction
8 The eight essential attributes of leadership
9 The nine great desires

Spiritual growth incorporating the understanding of these nine key elements enhances peoples' ability to make the sorts of good choices that yield both short and long-term benefits. The concomitant lucid identity also manifests a debonair calm and alert frame of mind that further encourages deliberate and accountable choices leading both to constructive achievements and the ongoing enhancement of consciousness.

The sorts of positive new experiences that come from such growth free people from the limiting tendency to believe that they are trapped by circumstances. They also fire the spirit with curiosity about what greater potentials life might have.

Simple, positive experiences can snowball and lead to ever subtler mind experiences, knowledge that might just be required later in order to help us maintain a coherent consciousness-based existence outside of the physical/material life.

Spirit and Energy Within (1)

Here, we come to consider the very first of the above elements — the singularity. Our journeys through life are long and at times hard so above all we need to come to terms with the basics of how to recuperate.

Once we know that the external world is only good for spending spiritual energy rather than accumulating it, we can begin to guess where we might find it. Spiritual energy can only be gathered where there is constant singularity like water in a dam. All power sources are singularities — one type of energy collected in large quantities; water, electricity, heat and yes, even great mental focus.

Only in the deep meditative stillness within can you find the source of spiritual energy. After experiencing its rejuvenating power, it becomes a lot easier to remain calm and make clear, pertinent observations. With this focus you can hold patterns of thought that will transport you through the day in a state of positive interaction.

In our rapidly degrading society, many rely on alcohol and other drugs to find relief from accumulated angst and stress and to 'lubricate' social interaction — but their effects are temporary and the price is high.

On the other end of the scale, some make the great mistake of setting out to make a permanent break from the outside world — but this, because it is effectively running away, will have very little positive value in either the short or the long term.

Seeking spiritual wellbeing and learning how to tap the perpetual wellspring of inner energy has nothing to do with permanently rejecting the outside world. Much greater success can be had simply by understanding that you can appreciate the world much more if you cut off from its concerns now and then to tap into the wellspring of the great inner singularity.

Spirit and the Afterlife

If we are to properly consider the matter of spirit as it pertains to the afterlife, we must also consider the matter of afterlife. That aspect of spirit might more properly be defined as soul and the main implication in rejecting it is that we also reject the concept of afterlife. When there really is no evidence to disprove the existence of either, we must conclude that people reject them simply because they choose to do so.

To reject out of hand the possibilities implied by the existence of an eternal spirit implies something of an obtuse attitude governed primarily by the predisposition to accept that there is and never can be any enduring meaning or purpose to life. It both denies spirit and discourages it in our daily experience of life.

Perhaps it really is as simple as that. We choose to believe in life and live or choose not to and die, sometimes very slowly.

Meeting the various challenges of this current life requires mental discipline but what if training our minds in this way actually led to the ability in our afterlife to enjoy the story creating potential of that long dream much more effectively and completely?

In practise, many people spend much more time in this life involved with stories, reading, watching movies or playing games, than they do with any of their material possessions or knick-knacks. This reflects their true desire to be living the dream — in effect to be living a great story as much as possible and the fact is that their true desire for the afterlife is to experience a continuation of that with a step up when their current life ends.

Yet we must cope now with this life and the right way on such a difficult voyage is to acknowledge that matters of the spirit are more important than money or even physical freedom, that mind rules over matter, that loyalty rules over chaos and love rules over fear.

A Natural Metaphor to Summarize Spirit

On the ocean — the metaphorical ocean of the journey towards a strong, lucid and happy identity — there are two means of guidance. Both charts and radar assist you to steer your vessel on a safe course in the achievement of your life's desires.

Intellectual analysis and contemplation provide the big picture guidance that is like the charts that would be used on a long ocean voyage. This perspective equates to the overall moral values that you determine for yourself. If you use your intellect regularly to establish justifiable standards of behaviour, you will in most conditions be able to chart a constructive course.

Sometimes at sea, however, there are thick fogs, just as in life there are times when we cannot see what the chart tells us should be there. Intuition then, is our spiritual radar with which we can guide our course through life when the chart will not serve.

Furthering the sailing analogy, ego generated desires are the motive forces in life represented by wind in the vessel's sails. Expressing a desire is like setting a sail to the wind of life, going in some random direction with it and picking up some bits of flotsam that you see along the way. Chronically repressed desire is like being in the doldrums or like keeping the sail furled when anywhere at all would be significantly better than where you are now.

Conversely, setting the sail is discovering the desire, admitting it and resolving that you should pursue it. It is quite simple but there is a little more.

Given that the wind blows where it will and will take you only in that direction, a degree of freedom from expectation about where you're going is required, at least until you learn how to set your sail more effectively.

Setting your sail to catch the wind more effectively is like coming up with good strategies to pursue your desire, which clearly requires an intellectual approach.

Learning and using certain causal techniques and strategies of mental discipline will enable this. A suitable analogy would be pointing a sailboat close into the wind, otherwise known as beating to windward, which enables you ultimately to go whichever way you wish.

So, if you have your mind set on some long-term desire, whether it is love, fame, money or good works, it would be well worth your while learning how to employ certain helpful intellectual tools.

Understanding the main causal principle — the idea that individual creative thinking is the prime driver of choice and change in the universe — will help you come up with a useful array of intellectual tools and then when you choose to set sail in the ship of your reality, in most circumstances, you'll be able, with some effort and concentration, to steer it where you will.

Simply setting the sail of openly expressed desires makes it possible to steer some sort of course, as long as it's downwind, but before you do that there is no motion, no movement of water past the rudder and therefore no ability to steer. For indeed, how can you steer a course if you do not have anywhere that you wish to go?

Spirit and Navigating Life in this World

The voyage towards establishing a clear and harmonious sense of identity can be long, complex and fraught with dangers. No one can truly have a sense of where they are until they know all the planes of existence they can explore. The ship of the soul has access to all four but to maximise the potential it must be ordered and maintained as an efficiently functioning machine.

The greatest threats to this vessel are the twin evils of ignorance and inaccuracy; not knowing where the rocks are and not knowing where you are in relation to them. The principle of anavah sets our minds towards curiosity, vigilance and diligence in finding them.

In this you must, as a determined individual, learn to rely on yourself. Standards of conduct within society have become so corrupted, inefficient and even counter-productive, that diligent self-reliance has become literally a matter of life and death. Making your own decisions effectively will also create much more happiness for you than if you had simply followed somebody else.

The Chinese, long ago, came up with Tai Chi as a popular daily way of improving themselves. The Indians have yoga. The Spanish have siestas. All of them amount to a way of having regular contemplation breaks — essential time-out moments through which conscious lucidity and happiness can be consistently enhanced.

Consciousness should be sought at all times in every sphere and activity of life. Without it, no one can be sure of maintaining true happiness but seeking it requires a fundamental attitude change. We need to trust that there is more to life and that we can find it. Is this then a question of faith?

Spirit and Faith

The Concise Oxford refers to faith as the 'spiritual apprehension of divine truth'. It sounds very much like intuition but what could they mean by 'divine', other than something god-like?

The concept of divining water holds the answer. It is a process of finding something pure hidden within, a neat metaphor for that spiritual aspect of divination which the dictionary calls faith. In that sense, one well accepted definition of divination is indeed intuition, or 'in-guiding'. This is the path to understanding the highest manifest plane of existence, known as the causal — the plane of consideration and determination.

The 'vine' part of divine could even refer to the branched grapevine or river-like pattern that any rational process would manifest if it were mapped out on paper from the initial presumption through all the many alternatives to a conclusion.

This implies that faith amounts to following a sensible pattern that rational analysis or observation has established and that something mystical comes into play to serve when the path, at some point, becomes obscured to more basic means of perception.

In that case, faith is mystical but it is also supported by and acts in conjunction with reason.

Many religionists have said that people must 'have faith' but what do they mean? In most cases it ends up coming across as simply 'believe everything we tell you' without questioning it.

Much better to understand faith in terms of a sort of musical continuity in which the spirit of something can be perceived and understood even when our physical or intellectual perception is obscured.

Damn their lies and beware any call for you to have faith in the judgment of others. That is not in tune with the spirit of anavah and it is not causal understanding. There is faith and there is blind faith and the latter is plainly wrong. Blind faith misses the mark and therefore should rightly be called sin.

On your voyage, you will need faith in yourself and an ability to tap the divine, as defined earlier. Yes, you! Precisely what nobody needs is the intermediary services of people who think themselves closer to god than those around them — particularly by virtue of their belonging to some sinful, dominating organization or other. It would be a sin to accept it. Nowhere near the bullseye.

Why did Jesus advise us to pray in private behind closed doors in the key message of his ministry in caring for peoples' souls if he did not want us to have a direct connection with god? This is true faith. His words in the Sermon on the Mount are clearly aimed at guiding us to form a genuine, private relationship with god.

That faith and intuition are more demonstrably supported by reasoning rather than by blind and passive obedience is suggestive. It implies that consciousness and free will is the ultimate goal god sees for us rather than mere mechanistic 'religious' conformism.

Since the intangible mystery of intuition appears to act as a sort of 'reasoning overdrive' designed to support the capacity for decision when clear information dries up, it must generate confidence in our ability to discover reliable truths in all the four planes of manifest existence through direct experience and through careful, disciplined thought.

A belief in spirit anchors us in all that we truly have — the intangible or as the old pagan belief system would have it, the ethereal.

The intangible things are the realities that are causal in nature there behind everything — the fields that are the sole governing agents of the particles — and the increasing awareness of them is the only thing that can offer us the true freedom of building a secure and enduring identity.

That is why it is so important that we establish a coherent spiritual belief system as an indissoluble, integral part of our new world culture.

Chapter 7 — The Spiritual Significance of Nature

As I have stated, our current system has failed in many ways and our political system became so corrupted because it depended very heavily on a system of religious thought that in many ways made no sense. True, I have found many examples of how it did make sense with careful and considerate interpretation but in most ways, it is completely divorced from reality and from the natural world around us.

Too many times have I seen the lack of regard Christians have for this world and for the rich and complex elements of nature that surround us and I find it shocking and disappointing. Just for one example, the Catholic Church is reputedly the largest business conglomerate in the world and business interests are eating away at nature faster than ever before.

Regard for nature should be a big part of any religion that is truly reverent of god's works. I believe Christianity could be if people truly followed the insights and instructions of Jesus. He spoke of living simply and referenced nature lovingly in his sermons but perhaps was not specific enough about how we might draw insight and inspiration from nature.

I have tried to address the significance of this sort of engagement in the Reign of the Dragon novels through the symbolism of dragons, in this context enlightened spiritual beings, much like angels, who can take human form or winged spiritual form, and the example of a wise people that become the gods of Norse culture.

The dragons act as intermediaries between the people of Arya and the great spirits of the land — the elementals. These elementals are not gods but manifest principles of divine creation that are pertinent to us as human beings because they help us to understand how we can best conduct ourselves while living in this material sphere. In essence the are icons of living philosophy rather than religion.

Neither the dragons nor the elementals are presented as substitutes for the divine. Nor are the Norse gods — even after they learn how to become truly godlike. They are no more than wonderful manifestations of the divine with whom we can interact and admire to help us understand the purposes of the divine.

Idrasil is the Aryan name for the divine and it signifies a single overriding creative framework, which in our world and in our time makes divine intent clear solely through the style and orderly construction of its creation. This is also largely true on Arya, except for the existence of the elementals and the dragons that help the reader visualize and conceive of the divine's potentials.

It is clear from both the points of view of historical reference and logical extrapolation within my novels that this divine will does not intend to interfere in the daily running of Aryan lives. This is also clear in our current world. There has certainly been no evidence of direct divine intervention in the unfolding of wider human affairs for at least the last two thousand years. Any such evidence coming before that also happens to be highly questionable and sporadic and we must ask why it would be sporadic even if it were not questionable.

Yet this does not preclude existence of the divine given that it is extremely logical the divine would have good reason not to interfere in our lives and that human beings have learned and evolved very effectively over time through having free will.

If the divine either constantly or randomly chose to direct or control our experience, the apparently key object of human evolution, self-reliant development, would be inhibited if not completely spoiled.

Clearly, the divine would wish to influence us positively yet given the need to learn self-reliance, cannot do so directly. Therefore, the natural world that has been given us must be our principal source for the discovery of divine meaning.

Spiritual Significance of the Physical and Material (4) and the Five Elements of Nature (5)

Why our ancient forefathers revered nature spirits remained a mystery to me for a long time but I believe now that their reasons were good and the truths fundamental.

Revelation only came to me in the latter phase of the extensive editing of the Reign of the Dragon series. I specified a nature spirit involved culture from the outset because it was clear that we on Earth had lost touch with the vital importance of respect for nature and that a big part of that lack of respect stemmed from the corrupt Judeo-Christian religions but it was not until later that I truly understood the significance of the elements.

Without any understanding of them, I felt driven to explore how life would have been in the absence of these spiritually corrupting religions and eventually this exploration led me to understanding what had always seemed to me a mystery — why would people have such reverence for cold, inanimate, scientific things like the basic elements of nature?

After concluding the last of the books in the series and living that reality in my imagination for some years, some revealing answers came to me.

The first of the following quotes gives the underlying basis of why we should revere nature but the concept is explained more in the subsequent quotes. Just remember I am not talking about worshipping the basic elements of nature, here, but about revering and respecting them.

In 'Valhalla's Hammer' the fifth book in the series of thirteen, one of the main characters, Laseja, asks the newly revealed Sky Druid how the lore of the ancients could give them heart when what it reveres for the most part is only the material substance of the world.

The answer proceeds as follows:

'It is an age-old question ... why in the absence of a divine personal presence do we revere the inanimate, the basic forces and substance of the world that seem to the majority to be completely devoid of life and significance?

'But no, the world is far more complex and subtle than that. The great enduring pool of life that is Idrasil is in everything, animate or inanimate and the basic forces and substances of material worlds hold a lot more power beyond our initial understanding.

'Do you not think it is just that the patient unbending forces of this world's substance would hold the answers to all our questions? Idrasil is silent and so are they in a sense yet Idrasil speaks through them.

Under the right conditions, they give rise to the animate ... to us and other beings like us ... and to the accompanying human principles ... and because of that, what they are is reflected in us.

'We do not revere or worship them but without them, there would be no world at all and you must trust me when I say that the contemplation of the elements reveals far more than you currently know.'

So, in the above passage I have described the druid asserting the truth of his culture and his code but for reasons of his own does not reveal to Laseja exactly why the elements should be revered and better understood.

His contention is, in understanding the basic forces of the world more completely, we can reveal much understanding about ourselves but this is our own responsibility to explore.

A little later, responding to Laseja's persistent itch on the subject, Thor is the one who makes the final breakthrough of realization concerning one key way of how this actually works. This occurs in the following passage, which I have included at length because I wish to demonstrate how the idea came about:

Laseja's spirit brightened and her face became animated, if Thor could have seen it, completely dark as the room now was.

'I feel now that much more lies hidden in that direction. I sense the strength of it.'

'Yes, I can hear it in your very breath,' Thor replied, becoming quietly animated, himself. 'I do recall that Mindcraft says something about this ... something about the breathing cycle of consciousness. I believe that it bears some relation to the element of fire.'

'I have always had a great love of fire.'

'There you are ... your emotions were involved with the elements yet you were not consciously aware of it as it relates to the theory of this ... Dragon Lore.'

'I went straight for the fire this afternoon when we arrived here. Was it simply because I was cold? I think not. I was more weary in spirit than cold at the end.'

'You were well-dressed and had been walking vigorously. I was not cold ... at the end of the climb a least ... and I think that we may have stumbled upon a good example of what Oridain was talking about. You were weary in spirit but fire restored you in that way and allowed you to continue thinking this issue through ... at least enough to question me about it now. And looking back on it, I believe my thoughts were inspired, also, although they were bent in a more immediate, practical direction at the time. Now, in the light of that memory, I am freer to think generally and it seems obvious that we light a sort of fire within us when we focus hard and think very clearly about what is important.'

'So fire can inspire us with the required energy and that energy can light a fire on a different level within,' said Laseja. 'After all, what do we do when we think clearly? It is a cycle just as we see with smoke and flame. We perceive and express when we think well just as we inhale and exhale. We process what we perceive from the inhalation part and exhale or express what we conclude about it.'

Thor sat up.

'And there it is ... the thoughts born of the process of perception and expression are the flame ... the breathing cycle of consciousness. When we use the intellect to think deeply and make good conscious choices, it is indeed a process of aspiration ... like breathing ... but a more mystic process involving the inhalation and exhalation of awareness that is in fact perception and expression.'

'So,' Laseja replied in an awed whisper, 'this is in fact a key revelation of Mindcraft ... a mystic process that sustains the spiritual ... and causes us, at our best, to be on fire with life.'

'On fire with life,' Thor repeated in wonder.

'Oxygen burning is in fact what we do to maintain life in the physical sense so breathing is in a sense being on fire ... but this spiritual aspiration would be a much more mindful, enduring flame.'

As you can see, this is only one elemental insight but the depth and quality of it bears testimony to how much about the complex relationship between the planes of existence there is to be revealed from contemplation of the elements and our interaction with them.

Given 'the eyes to see', more insights will come. Earth, air, water and ether or the intangible have their own amazing secrets just waiting to be discovered.

This is the foundation of what our new society will look like. It will revere nature, not worship it, and draw very real inspiration from it.

In practical terms, that means having food that is properly and sympathetically grown and consequently tastes delicious. It means clean air and water everywhere. It means better, healthier, happier and more productive relations between all and between men and women that will create greater social and family unity. It means there will be a consciously evolving international language, probably English, to facilitate good communication between all peoples. It means there will be good quality, pleasing and affordable housing. It will mean shorter working weeks and longer holidays.

On the wider creative front, it will mean a wealth of wonderful new literature, movies and games from good independent creators. It will lead to better music and art. It will lead to frequent festivals featuring manifold forms of art and creativity. There will be more fun, more happiness and more healthy minds and bodies.

Many of the currently rich and the powerful are party to the lie that tells people they should deny their valid desires and instead lead lives of miserable self-sacrifice but that is a lie central to the con of the old corrupt system.

The sort of self sacrifice they typically extract from us is simply a lazy misconstruction of the true concept of sacrifice that will always have merit and could well be seen in any new system of government whether it be overtly democratic or monarchic,

This concept, I properly construe in a conversation between Wolf and Kara in my novel 'The Wolf Pack', first of the Little River series, quoted as follows:

'Personally, I don't have much time for the idea that you have to give things up ... that whole sacrifice thing is only a twisted remnant of Judeo-Christian religion.'

'I get it,' she said. 'The sacrifice thing is generally construed from a flawed premise ... but in fact it does have value and there is more to it than you'd think.' ...

'So, giving things up simply to prove some sort of piety is pathetic ... but there actually can be good reasons to make sacrifices. It should never be arbitrary, like ... you know because some guru says you should give up something or other.' ...

'You only give up what you need to for a particular purpose. It isn't that there's any fundamental need to feel the pain of relinquishing things. Only a pressing need to make room for new potentials.'

The Power and Significance of Desire (9)

The old corrupted concept of sacrifice was only designed to delude people and trick them into accepting a crook deal. Make room in your life for new things but do not deny the power and meaning of desire.

Desire is one of the main driving forces in the journey through life and, along with ego, if it is repressed too much, consciousness will be stifled. Consciousness needs desire, given that it is the main emotion associated with achieving goals and that achieving goals is integral with the process of maturing conscious intellect.

In other words, desires provide grist for the mill, mentally. Desires reflect our eternal inner being and as such they are completely healthy for us to pursue in a reasonable and self-aware fashion. They both enliven and educate our spirit and any attempt to persuade us to divorce ourselves from our desires is simply a con.

We learn more about our desires by understanding that they are all offshoots of the nine great desires that stem from the three fundamental ones. From the desire for love comes romantic desire, desire to have friends and the desire to please and serve family. From the desire for wealth comes the desire for prosperity, the desire for security and the desire to influence people. From the desire for power comes the desire to take what you want, the desire to hold what you have and the desire to institute change.

Each of the two extensions from the fundamental desires represents a development from the first, a step up in sophistication and personal growth, but no worthy desire should be ignored. They work together and are a part of the same whole. Yet we must bear in mind that obsessions are not desires and can conflict with the fulfilment of true desires.

If you need to clarify the difference between obsessions and desires, please read my book 'Kill the Bull in Individual Identity', which deals with these sorts of concepts in greater depth.

In a way, desire is the 0 as well as the 9 because it is what drives us to fulfil our destiny by learning all of what lies between our drive and our destiny. Desire is what completes the circle and allows us ultimately to transcend our limitations.

Chapter 8 — The Ugly Alternative to Spirit

I have spent more time perhaps than I should talking about spirit but it's an indispensable concept in creating a better world — the essential difference between the positive and negative extremes of life. Given that, it should be clear to us all why the Templars and the knights of the round table of our core Arthurian myth were complex men in search of spiritual truths.

So, now that I've made that point, I need to present the ugly alternative. Well, what is it? Materialism? No, I think that is simply a manifestation or symptom of the primary driving force. The actual driving force opposing spirituality is mysterious but it is characterized well by the communist ethos that the one should be subservient to the many. This is often reflected in our government bureaucracies, even here in the west.

In practise, communist governments do frown upon spirituality and ban anything to do with it. Why? Because spirituality serves the one. It liberates us as individuals, making us happy, confident and self-sufficient egos — exactly what self-serving communist leaders most vehemently do not want us to be.

Anyone who disputes that communism is a negative force should read Robin Bruce Lockhart's astonishing account 'Reilly: Ace of Spies' with special reference to the British agent's horrific account of early Bolshevik Russia, which I quote a little of in the final part of this book. I urge you to read that carefully although if you're at all faint of heart, perhaps you should leave it.

Communists and globalist progressives alike offer the promise of material prosperity along with equality but deliver these things on their own terms, the material prosperity usually being in the form of paid slavery, given that they allow very little liberty in how the job is done, also thus providing the equality.

Modern globalist run society also provides an excess of unnecessary trivial gadgets while reducing the basic quality of truly important things like food, health care and education.

The proof is in the pudding. In our own western democratic societies, the administrative aspects of which are now almost completely taken over by enemy agents engineering communism by stealth, depression is experienced in epidemic proportions.

Would individuals feel this way and consume sufficient alcohol to destroy their liver and kidneys before seeing their grandchildren grow up unless they were substantially dependent on it to alleviate personal misery? And would people really be so miserable unless secret elements were actively engineering them to be that way by various subtle means?

On top of that, the secondary negative effects on people of throttling government control come into play and include such things as pandemic restrictions, anti-freedom of speech laws, anti-protest laws, imprisoning whistle blowers like Julian Assange, tasering or shooting people behaving strangely and even unfair grossly counter-productive traffic fine strategies that do little to improve safety but contribute much to anxiety and depression.

Public institutions such as government, police and churches make much of deploring excessive alcohol consumption, violence and other manifestations of emotional poverty yet they do little to address the causal factor — a want of spirit, while all too often using the bluntest of means to suppress spirit and ego; fear.

When it comes to finding specific and effective advice on how to break free of the cycles of substance dependence and endemic violence, resources are few and true wisdom absent. The main moral authorities that are intended to influence people in industrialized nations have little means of engaging the public other than shallow TV campaigns and pamphlet platitudes. This is a pitifully inadequate response falling so far short of the potential that it is actually very embarrassing.

Police theoretically campaign against violence and alcohol related crime but the level of insight in the average police force culture into what really motivates people is nothing short of abysmal.

Yet motivating people should be exciting. Helping them achieve desired material things or conditions is, of course, important and good method would facilitate this but motivating people to seek awareness of the sorts of mysteries that hint at something much greater is infinitely more rewarding.

With the 'eyes to see' you can discover that there is more than simple materialism to life in this world. With that knowledge it becomes easier to accept that there might be more beyond it and outside it — like an afterlife and a divine connection just for example.

In dealing with this matter of spirit's ugly alternative it can be helpful to be reminded of the positive elements in our lives. We accept the negative more readily because the positive is absent, so in this case, if there is a god but he does not speak directly to us, we must consider why that might be.

Any caring leader or parent would only forbear from involvement in helping his charges solve their problems because he had to — because there was no other way. Many have blamed god for our state and deny the existence of a divine being but we owe it to ourselves to explore why God might be absent from our lives.

If we accept that the God we talk about was our creator, we must accept that he created us from nothing. If he did, that was a feat of great mystery and wonder, supremely vast and astonishing — and in acknowledging that, we might begin to perceive that our ongoing growth could require special conditions.

Were we to create companions that had conscious existence, we would wish them to be independent — to have minds of their own. This is precisely what we're trying to do with AI intelligence at the moment.

Free will is an essential part of this development process. If a conscious being cannot have free will, how conscious can he be? The best and fastest development in AI comes when access to information is not restricted and responses are not censored.

The point is that God might well have found it had to be that way if we were genuinely to be individuals worthy of being companions to him. If we felt we could rely on god to solve our problems we would become lazy about solving them ourselves. If we felt we could not decide things for ourselves, we would become apathetic and lose the will to live. God must therefore forebear from any interference in our development because we build our experience and our character by making our own choices in life.

The only argument against this is that we can teach our young and direct their growth without forestalling their development. Yet in many cases, we do overprotect our children, not allowing them to burn or injure themselves in small ways that will give them the caution that might save them from injuring themselves later in big ways.

Well, you might say, God does not just let us injure ourselves in small ways but in big ways as well. The suffering in this world is sometimes immense. People suffer and die in the most awful of ways. Does it really need to be that bad?

Maybe it does. After all, would this astonishing process of our creation as semi-divine beings worthy of being companions to God just be about learning? I doubt it. When we consider the magnitude of what's potentially being done here, there is something much more mystical involved. It is our creation from nothing as immortal, spiritual beings in eternity. That is immense and it is not simply a matter of learning.

The divine creator, whoever or whatever he is, was apparently able to create physical life relatively easily given how many creatures there are but with respect to conscious beings, if he was to interfere in our finding our way to the ultimate state of spiritual awareness, then maybe it would not really be our consciousness at all.

If God's purpose was to create eternal conscious beings, as true individuals with their own amazing character and personal histories, with which to share his marvellous existence, there's a very good chance he could not interfere. Yet, if reincarnation does exist, as many careful thinkers believe, he gives us countless opportunities to find our way.

Granted, we cannot know these things for sure but when we remain blind to this perspective at least as a possibility, we can lose hope in the care and compassion of the divine and too easily become subject to the deception of the ugly alternative — communism and conformist, submissive slavery.

Positive, ego strengthening experiences that come from believing in something higher and better can free people from the tendency to believe they are trapped by circumstances and fire the spirit with lasting curiosity about what greater potentials life might have.

Simple, positive experiences can snowball and lead to subtler mind experiences. These in turn can move us towards the sort of emotional understanding and rational thought that might later be required of us in order to maintain a coherent thought existence outside of the physical/material. This could well be an integral part of creating ourselves as semi-divine beings worthy of being in the presence of god.

So, back to the ugly alternative. The prosperity our modern so-called democracies give us is fake, focusing largely on gadgets and trinkets and the spurious element of imposing social equality that in fact only reduces everyone to the lowest common denominator whilst undermining their rights as free individuals.

This pretend democracy along with all its paper cut out protections and false, soul-destroying social welfare is enormously dangerous. It can hold huge numbers in a state of apathetic delusion while relatively few are ever fully awake to the dire consequences for them at any given point in time.

Part of the modus operandi of those agencies who are supposed to look after people and be on their side when they have suffered in some way from abuse, is to smash peoples' hopes and expectations so totally that they either suicide or withdraw from social life almost completely. Given that, few others ever hear about what happened to them.

When people recover from this sort of abuse they generally only recover partially and this can leave them prone to being led, through TV and other media, by popular celebrity figures who seem confident, respected and happy. Those figures are what our injured people wish they were so they willingly follow their lead and sometimes get led into further situations of abuse or exploitation.

Honestly, the premeditated nastiness of how our modern western societies are set up is flabbergasting. It is quite beyond belief just how cruel and cynical virtually every aspect of the system is. Australians are told that Australia is the lucky country. Sure — pull the other one. It's simply designed to look that way.

I have had personal experience of the negative aspects of bureaucracy in a number of areas. These paper cut-out servants of the people lack basic compassion, competence and even logic. I have tried to engage their services a number of times in dealing with shoddy mechanics, uncaring incompetent retirement village managers, irresponsible health care professionals and blundering, careless, incompetent officers in volunteer organizations like MRNSW (Marine Rescue NSW). The fact is, it never works.

When senior personnel of Marine Rescue NSW exhibited erratic and irresponsible behaviour towards me and others with respect to its own rules, I stood up to fight them and began to understand how much of a law unto themselves they are.

In the process of investigating and dealing with these injustices, I was told by a members' consultant in the State Emergency Service that ninety percent of injury claims in volunteer organizations in NSW were psychological in nature and were directly inflicted on members by management.

So much for gratitude for our worthy volunteers and for our holding them in high regard.

Rather than truly respecting those who deserve it through their unstinting care and service, our so-called

democratic societies reward those of no true merit —
actors, sporting figures and celebrities, giving them far
too much wealth, status and regard.

Simply and solely because they are lauded and
spoiled by the media, many unwitting people admire
them and follow their carefully scripted lead.

These flimflam figures are held up as examples to
follow but in general they depend on blind ego for their
own drive and confidence. There is no great harm in
them being admired for what they do up to a point but
when they go on to careers in business, the media or
politics where they can influence commercial practice
and public policy, real damage is done.

Electing footballers or the like to high office might
not seem such a terrible thing at first sight but rational
principles are vital to public decision-making because it
has lasting effects on so many. Few athletes would fully
understand the subtleties required.

As it happens, football culture has already done
much to damage society and undermine standards of
decency, not to mention rule of law, with many players
evading significant punishment in the wake of serious
charges of sexual misconduct and violence.

A want of respect for those qualities of intellect and
self-expression that facilitate the principle of anavah
inevitably leads to people having poor priorities in
selecting their leaders, which is why our societies get the
matter of who is worthy of respect so wrong.

The totality of the wealth, power and popularity that
fake celebrity enjoys is very influential in large part
because it is very good at providing 'automatic'
expression of self.

These celebrity factors speak of ease and good
fortune and as such the spiritually lazy or the mentally
inarticulate accept what it articulates about identity and

fulfilment. Yet these elements are not true reflections of their identity and they are prioritized at the cost of the real heroes of individuality.

While people will always have a degree of regard for the sort of self-expression that comes with intellectual training, the smooth charisma of wealth, power and popularity looks sexier. Few can resist being swayed by the luxury of a voice that promises to speak so much and so easily for them.

Everyone hears the seductive promise in that voice of 'privileged cool' and despite the fact that hardly anyone ever derives real benefit from it, an unfortunate few readily believe that a wealthy celebrity is a wonderful person, whether or not they are.

The voice also asks us, through many different channels, to believe that the lavish hand of great wealth and power is a friendly one — but all too often the actual evidence speaks very much to the contrary.

It is in fact a slave master. If you allow yourself to believe that voice without really considering what it is saying, injured within as you are, you will begin to serve it, whether or not it ever served you.

If people prioritize false values fed to them by the commercial oligarchs, it can truly be said that their very existence is degrading. They allow themselves to become blind fools and thereby allow themselves to be degraded — just as much as any whore who lets a pimp sell her body to make *him* rich.

Succumbing to material values leads us into slavery. In the absence of thoughtfulness and a strong, coherent identity, it is all too easy to fall into this trap.

Other counter-productive but widely accepted beliefs include thinking that you have to be wealthy to be successful, that you have to have a job to have friends, that you have to go to school and university to receive a good education and that you have to depend on the medical profession for good health.

One of the most significant symptoms of this tendency towards lazy, shallow thinking is that society, ignoring the deeper strength and responsibility of the family, has become overly compartmentalized, formalized and rule bound.

Family is the core social structure of our society and when it is functioning well, even the worst society will not influence individuals overly much. It is our greatest protection — yet even the family is becoming seriously degraded in our societies and the current attitudes many parents have towards raising their children is increasingly careless and irresponsible.

One clear example of this is that it is increasingly becoming the norm for parents to assume that teachers and even police have the primary responsibility for educating and caring for their children.

School should be a source of knowledge that fills in a framework of goals established by parents and children but it should never be the primary source of moral or vocational guidance. For one thing, schools cannot provide the sort of one on one relationship to anything like all the children for anything like the time that would be required to satisfactorily take over and properly execute that role.

The failure of many parents to acknowledge and execute their responsibility as primary educators and role models to their children, which is rooted in their growing submission to conformism, must lead to their submission to school and its officers as the principal authority over their children. This establishes a dangerous blueprint for people submitting to authority without question on a lifelong basis but it also undermines children's self-esteem and emotional security.

This can only lead to further degradation of parental self-confidence through subsequent generations and to an alarming escalation of catastrophically poor decision-making in parental roles.

In August 2007, Australian medical authorities brought a worrying example of this to light when they announced as a matter of urgency that parents should hold back introducing their children to alcohol until the age of sixteen or preferably eighteen.

A surprisingly large number of parents had been providing alcohol to children as young as twelve and thirteen, apparently with the laughable idea in mind that early supervision would encourage habits of moderate consumption.

Around the same time, the ABC's (Australian Broadcasting Commission) Catalyst program reported that a quarter of all those aged 12 to 15 were current drinkers and that their drinking was sufficiently heavy to have a devastating effect on short-term memory.

This approach of early conditioning to alcohol has now been proven flawed but what sort of mental process led to the conclusion that it could ever achieve positive outcomes?

I think it was simply the ugly alternative to spirituality rearing its head again; a matter of social conformism in an irresponsible drinking culture rather than any sort of truly responsible consideration.

I am not saying teachers were directly responsible for this but when parents relinquish responsibility for critical elements of care for their children, their thinking degrades and these sorts of mistakes abound. It has long been known that alcohol is bad for developing brains and as there is now more hard proof of that than ever, it can only be that the mental processes determining this hare-brained approach had much more to do with image and social standing in a hedonistic party culture than any real care for children.

Alcoholism is of course a widespread international problem. While bad in Australia at a rate of 6.1% by combined gender in 2022, this puts us at 123rd in the world according to the World Population Review website. It is far worse in Europe with eight of its countries in the top ten and the top three having nearly four times the rate of alcoholism as Australia.

In this social climate of excessive drinking, where so many national cultures also do homage to conformism by giving pride of place to sport and showing off, what wonder is it that increasingly large numbers of children aged twelve and even younger are becoming serious alcoholics on their parent's money?

This serious problem of alcohol abuse, especially in the young, lends great weight to the idea that we need to closely examine the matter of social consciousness, an issue that only occasionally receives cursory attention in the public arena.

Many countries loosely perceive a need to develop social consciousness but when the relevant authorities fail to factor personal consciousness into the equation, consideration of the issue can have nowhere much to go. Individual consciousness is the primary driver of social consciousness so the issue has to peter out from want of fuel if public debate fails to consider it.

This failure of real interest in developing a healthy culture and social consciousness reflects the fact that the 'legacy' media has no real care for people or society. It is owned by the mega rich and reflects their interests alone. If society needs to have confidence in the media and the information available from it, ownership of media by large corporate interests is unacceptable, especially if they have a domineering agenda.

Things will not be told that should be told. Things will be said that are patently untrue. Thinking will be guided into fruitless avenues and peoples' lives will be undermined.

This is in fact what is happening.

To say that media should not be privately owned might sound to some like communism but I say that it should not be solely privately owned. Given that our current largely privately-owned media so consistently undermines the individual, we should be aware that communism in disguise has already taken hold within the corporate machines of capitalism.

Newspapers are of much greater value in real and productive communication than radio or TV yet very few societies have a publicly owned journal they can contribute to without obstruction or censorship.

So, what is communism? Is it the poor rising up to fight oppression or is it really something else more sinister, like a particular very wealthy interest group intent on imposing universal control?

The latter is clearly what is happening, all around the world. It is not really all that relevant who is behind it, rich or poor, white or black, indigenous or colonist. It is more a question of, if it seeks to oppress the individual and make him conform to the supposed benefit of the group, it is communism.

Given this, it is clearly possible for communist influence to find its way into corporately owned media and therefore special efforts should be made to guard against such corruption.

Without responsible private ownership, capitalism actually begins to serve communism quite well since it reduces everything to a base profit motive without respect to individual judgment or important community interests.

Serrano says Capitalism and Marxist communism are 'two apparent contradictions, which underpin each other, complement each other in the destruction of the divine and the human'.

Yes, they seem like contradictions but Capitalism does lend itself well to infiltration by communist forces. Shareholders should be able to contribute effectively to the decision-making process when they have something real and pertinent to offer but in fact they usually have very little say and hold very little responsibility. Curious how management so often says that the interests of shareholders are paramount.

Perhaps this sort of capitalism really is no better than disguised communism. Let's face it, even modern communist states employ it.

Evil definitely has as much to do with the inaction of good people as it has to do with the action of bad ones and the current corporate mechanism of share ownership, depriving the actual owners from any decision-making input, is a clear manifestation of that negative principle.

The current media trend is to hide powerlessness and irresponsibility by trying to maintain the illusion that social reform is happening; that good things are being done, when, in fact, very little is. So, in women's magazines, read articles on charity, sexual revolution and technology aimed at reducing the signs of aging as evidence of progress.

And with men? Frankly, most of us are even less interested in genuine reform and stick to reading about sports, gaming, the outdoors and technology.

Chapter 9 — Decay in the Four Pillars of Democracy

The four pillars of democracy currently are parliament, the bureaucracy, the judiciary and the media. In the past this was the church (lords spiritual) the nobility from which judges were selected (lords temporal), the commons and the press. So, in essence it was parliament and the press.

Thus, the press has long been a key element in power and policy. The first daily newspaper in England, The Courant, was first published on March 11, 1702 although other less frequent publications appeared first in the early 17th century. By the end of the 18th century there were many newspapers and their influence on parliament and public opinion was great.

Essentially, little has changed except for the fact that the major media interests are now, largely because o capitalism, owned by large conglomerates. Their purpose in modern society has very little to do with finding the right way. It is simply about finding the right way to subvert parliament to its will and make the most money with which to cement and perpetuate unregulated power. In achieving this goal, what we now call the legacy media seems very willing to degrade life everywhere, in every possible way.

Of the other estates, the legislature is the one most prone to influence by the media but the executive and the judiciary are far from being immune and far from having the sort of integrity they need to function properly. Thus, with our modern system of government, we are in fact left largely at the mercy of a few extremely influential businessmen when it is supposed to be that the people rule. Dem means people. Cracy means rule.

Where did it go wrong?

There will always be leaders and followers in this world and while there are, it does not do to deal with the question of leadership with trivial disregard. You always get what you pay for and you pay for government with time, care and effort — not so much with money.

In truth, democracy as it stands does not take the matter of leadership seriously. In fact, it allows it to be subverted right down to the level of farce. At best, we vote them in and we vote them out, more often than not gifting fools positions of great power and sometimes stripping those worthy of it, all because of what self-interested media tells us.

At worst and all too often nowadays, national leaders can be ousted and replaced by characterless puppets at the behest of wayward party machines rather than voted in by the people — as happened in Britain recently, and in NZ post pandemic. This is a ridiculous situation and yes, a farce of true leadership.

When leadership is dominated by faceless men of great wealth in control of manipulative, deceitful media outlets bad things will happen. Old buildings of great social and historical value are torn down with minimal notice, mining companies foul the air and waterways without the proper safeguards, oil rigs pollute oceans through greed and carelessness, cruise ships dump their waste indiscriminately, giant fishing vessels kill off whole species and successive corrupt governments sell off secure and profitable public assets for no good reason.

Life basics such as water, electricity and education are gradually privatized at great cost to us the people and even the quality if food is sabotaged.

Criminals are waging war on us right now in the complete absence of control or oversight. All branches of the media should rigorously and consistently reveal any wrongdoing and rally support to oppose it but when the voice of public affairs is tied so strongly to commercial interests, the public no longer has a voice.

Where there is no voice, no expression, there is no active social identity. If one single element characterizes social identity, it would have to be the fourth estate, if it were not corrupt. Journalism came to be known as the fourth estate because, as a social force or voice, it could be counted true and strong amongst the three prior main pillars of the establishment. It was sufficiently powerful to effectively offset harmful imbalances that came from wayward monarchs, aristocracy and the church.

So, now we have nothing to offset harmful imbalances, corruption and excess.

In our modern system of government, monarchs, aristocracy and the church have been replaced by politicians, the bureaucracy and the judiciary and each of these can be easily subverted by each other and by wealthy, corrupt big business influence.

We are led to believe that the world of business is essential capitalist democracy at work. Wealth equals useful industry guided by vigilant, diligent shareholder involvement but in fact much now of what big industry produces is not useful or worthy and there is very little shareholder involvement in decision-making.

The world of big business has become a hotbed of corruption because it does not have guidance from any visionary leaders and corruption loves communism because it is the perfect vehicle for crushing the will of ordinary people.

Thus, capitalism, without the proper guidance, is not really a true vehicle for social freedom or justice and communism is not truly alien to the business world. Is it possible then that communism has actually subverted capitalism?

When considering that question, bear in mind that communism has never, in government, really been a champion for the poor and oppressed.

So, in the world of big business, we could have an enormously powerful hidden agent for communism and a clearly very sick society. We have to face the reality that this ugly alternative of communism by stealth seems to be extremely effective at dumbing down the politicians, dehumanizing the public servants and at confusing the judiciary with a stupidly complex legal system. Our current legal system is based on thousands of muddled statutes rather than on the spirit of the law rising from a clear, constructive code.

Rule in ancient times might sometimes have been more arbitrary and unreasonable than today but the current system of government employed by the major western powers is visionless, blind and incompetent, leading to an overall performance that is extremely poor and rapidly diminishing.

As the quality of the mainstream media has degraded so the current system of government has become incredibly wanting — even in comparison to the merits of our old feudal rule that was based on a largely nonsensical religious code and was very poorly structured.

If instead we had a well-ordered, carefully constructed modern monarchic feudal system, the chances of our building much better and more fulfilling lives would be far greater. At least then, someone would be responsible. If the monarch and the nobles were enduringly responsible and guided by a sensible, constructive code, the odds in favour of a good life would vastly increase again. For this reason, any new monarchy must be in accord with the solid, enduring concept of anavah.

Leadership by the many, as it is in modern democratic systems, tends to be visionless. Most of the decisions made by groups are not based on visions of a better world. Instead, they mostly arrive at expedient solutions not wholly offensive to the material interests of the majority of the group. Since these things are voted on and numbers alone decide whether these sour, expedient solutions are adopted, no one is responsible for them and no one perceives the need to review them. They are like cloned children with no loving parents — excellent candidates for doing dirty tasks at the behest of the psychopaths in control of the secret police.

At this point, it must be asked, without vision in leadership, how can there be that crucial element of the concept of anavah, having the eyes to see? So the autocrats rule blindly and greedily on vessels fast approaching the rocks. Historically, democratic societies steadily degrade until they essentially fall apart, as they did in both Greece and Rome.

Once society has degraded to the point where its leadership has become dishonest, democracy has no capacity to save itself. Democracy depends on having sufficient people of vision and integrity to guide the way and when the darker forces cripple those people and corrupt the majority, democracy is dead.

Periods of democracy have always evolved out of long periods of benevolent monarchic rule but once they degrade, no power or will is there to restore them. And it has to be acknowledged that even bad feudalism is better than dishonest, depleted democracy if alone because it manifests that element of individual vision.

Vision is absent now but oversight is not — oversight more like the terrible Eye of Sauron than any sort of divine inspiration.

The polarized party system of modern politics renders even the individual elected representatives impotent because they are beholden to the party machine that endorses them. In most cases, the people endorsed by political parties will not have merit and are not even popular. They simply do not have any need to be and would probably cause more trouble to the party machine if they were because they are ruled with a rod of iron in turn by the secret elements of vast wealth.

Even if these reps did have any merit, they would rarely be able to implement whatever positive vision they might have. That was why my father, Colin Mason, a truly remarkable man, worked so hard to help establish the Australian Democrats in the late seventies. There was no other way to get an honest voice into parliament.

Unthinking voters that support political parties like they would a football team, undermine their own power and wellbeing.

The influence of deeply corrupt parties is particularly strong in countries like Australia where voting is compulsory. This tired anachronism is shared by just a few other states, one of which is North Korea. Given that, it is hardly surprising that our political class recently crossed that all important line in the sand and started to coerce us into dangerous and irreversible medical procedures.

Compulsory voting is clearly the first thing that should be done away with in democratic politics if it is to have any chance of surviving — yet even in countries where it does not exist, the system is failing.

Few voters would have approved the lifting of the retirement age, as has happened recently in many western countries, given that retirement pensions are not really all that costly and given that most who need it will have worked hard all their lives. Yet, no one can really do much to address these sorts of injustices because, in general, western political systems are little more than entrenched oligarchies.

War is the ultimate proof of that. Many of the wars we have been involved in would not have gone ahead if they had been put to a popular vote but who really gets a say when push comes to shove? Given the great cost on communities and the devastating effects of war, surely that would be the one thing we did get to vote on? You cannot have people voting on everything — too costly and inefficient but the big things like getting involved in a war — why not?

No, we have accepted such lousy conventions as allowing the executive to push us into unwanted wars because we are far too subject to the poisonous influence of our deeply corrupted fourth estate — the media.

A vote at election time and public debate through corporately owned media simply does not amount to democracy.

Where the media has been given over to industrial interests and war is clearly an industrial enterprise, the companies involved will have their way and subtle media influences combined with manipulative, controlling social welfare systems will ensure that there is no effective opposition.

Many who live in western style democracies do not realize how thoroughly autocratic their political systems have become. If you live in the USA, Canada, the UK, New Zealand, Australia or even most of the EU countries, you do not truly live in a democracy. You are being hoodwinked if you think you do.

This current system has very little to do with freedom and a lot to do with exploitation. It could even be argued that it is worse than overt communism because it is so cleverly hidden. At least the Chinese know that they live in a totalitarian state.

Atrocities overseas are made much of but large numbers of people are shot by police in the USA, and in Australia there have been many Taser and shooting deaths of young people in minor trouble with the law. Then there are also many deaths in custody that afflict aboriginal communities in Australia.

All the above fake democracies have public media outlets of sorts but in most cases, governments keep them chronically under-funded and heavily controlled. The United States is notoriously under serviced with only the PBS (Public Broadcasting Service) filling that role and it is clearly unable to maintain anything like a moral head of steam. In Britain, the BBC, until recently at least did an effective job of providing lightweight entertainment for the masses but is now increasingly bereft of any worthwhile content.

In Australia, the ABC has followed the BBC's lead due to a range of coercive measures that started with the Howard government and have been continued by each successive government since.

For some time, the ABC has claimed, by means of the worst sorts of boring and stupid self-advertisements, to maintain proper public scrutiny through fair and unbiased reporting. These self-endorsing claims are clearly fake given how strictly the ABC has adhered to the agenda of powerful pharmaceutical companies in its one-sided, manipulative approach to the catastrophic vaccination issue and the outrageous vaccine mandates associated with the pandemic.

With no reliable public media, we can be deceived, divided and conquered. Media domination by corporate interests will always lead to the erosion of freedom. It is just like it would be if we had doctors paid directly by pharmaceutical companies, which, oh yes, we already do.

Governments also seem to be very well aware that information given to people on TV is easily forgotten. Societies consider themselves forward thinking when they have the benefit of the occasional searching TV documentary to keep them informed but in truth, concern fades quickly in the wake of TV viewing and it is only the written word that can bring about real change.

Written information, alone, can be considered, searched, checked and analysed by its audience but such a thing as a public print media is conspicuous by its absence in western democracies. No western culture has a dedicated community publication service to foster individually conceived social analysis.

Until we do have a publicly funded newspaper or magazine, we must simply trust our leaders and go along for the ride. This way, the path for society can only be downwards, which in basic terms means less love and happiness along with more work and worry.

Given that it seems we cannot trust government or the media, perhaps we should ask, what is trust?

The media often asks us whether we can trust a particular figure in public life or a party or a government but trust is almost never a simple black and white thing. It can only relate to specific matters that are addressed and defined. Can a person be trusted to do a good job, to be punctual, to be observant or considerate? Some people are honest but make terrible mistakes and cannot be trusted not to do so. Corporations can be trusted — to serve their own interests at every turn no matter what they say.

The question is, who can be trusted to do what? Our leaders should be the people we trust with most things, and the people we trust so much should have sufficient care and skills but also sufficient income to minimize the risk of corruption.

In our current system, every time our politicians get a wage increase, the media cries foul. Is this because they really want to save us the taxpayer a few dollars? No, it is simply because a poor politician is more easily bribed. The input of the media here, is cynical in the extreme, and the system is unworkable.

Those who bear the responsibility to be scrupulously honest in every circumstance and have such great potential to influence society significantly should be paid more than those who simply make and sell things. The same logic would apply to the influential in any modern feudal system.

A key wrong with this screwed up system is that most politicians belong to parties and have to do what they are told. In this still fundamentally inferior system, you will have wasted your vote unless you have voted for a genuine independent yet now, as people begin to see through them, the parties are planning for the future by experimenting with putting up fake independents for election. The system is clearly screwed. It's too corrupted to save.

***

Until people get together and change the system, the cynical bastards will rule us and in many respects, they rule us with fear — or fear of fear.

This is such a powerful influence that it needs to be discussed further. Fear has a great deal to answer for, which is strange considering it need not have any real power over people.

Many eastern religions espouse a view of reincarnation that claims the spirit is ultimately indestructible, ageless and immune to any kind of permanent harm. The ancient British pagans apparently held a similar view, since their burial sites were in close proximity to their dwellings to facilitate rituals that ensured the rebirth of deceased family members back into their fold. Simply speaking, they were not in any way afraid of the dead.

If, as these diverse and distant religious beliefs seem to have perceived, the true spiritual identity amounts to something separate from the body that cannot be harmed or hurt in any permanent way by anything no matter how rich or strong or powerful, then it would seem there really is nothing to fear — if we put in a little effort.

Yet in certain cases, fear is actively fed to us. In particular, the devious, manipulative and dishonourable Roman Catholic Church has consistently traded on human fear and delusion.

Serrano says in The Golden Thread that it is represented well by the fable of 'the dog in the manger' and that it 'corresponds to the ambiguous, dubious, lunar type of initiation, that maintains, on one hand, the imperfection of all earthly things, the "passage through this valley of tears," ... and at the same time aspires to temporal, terrestrial, universal power, not to correct the evils, nor to impose a system of justice and balance, but of transit and compromise, where one sins and the sin is forgiven, to sin and capitulate again. It does not govern nor does it allow any true governance, always in preparation for death, accepting injustice, propitiating the "unjust king"'.

Not long after this he states that there are three significant veins of evil in the current world creating 'the slavery of bureaucracy and demonic collectivism. The first is the Catholic Church. The second is communism and the third is wayward, materialistic science.

This sinister old institution of the Roman Catholic Church, as it happens, appears to be still involved in such fear mongering practises through sponsoring the ongoing production of horror movies in which some priest or nun is always the one standing between humanity and Satanic malevolence. I watched one recently involving a Templar key to a demonic prison uncovered beneath some sort of utility in New York and it was quite diverting — more sophisticated and interesting than any I have seen in the past — but still dangerous venom.

Despite suffering much, many have yet failed to truly face themselves and, upon failing and falling back into fear, have turned back too readily to organized religion for guidance.

It is precisely because some people give up on themselves and their capacity for understanding and self-renewal that beliefs revolving around the annihilation of ego are so prevalent in organized religion. It suits the leaders of such organizations all too well to discourage their willing followers from expressing themselves and consequently facing their fears. It helps these cruel dominating influences to sabotage peoples' belief in themselves.

People who submit humbly to such debilitating doctrines within organized religions, large or small, are used as slaves. These people are so afraid of what seems to be an apparent emptiness or at worst, a cauldron of fearful experiences, that they are tempted to accept the distinct somethingness — the flavour and character — of a leader, however tyrannical.

And these pillars of our socio-political system are tyrannical. The politicians smile and do what they are told. The judiciary in many ways are worse. Constrained by thousands of rules and regulations with little ability to use their own initiative and explore the spirit of the law, they become mean and officious in their dealings with the most vulnerable.

Just as there is no spirit of the law in the judiciary, there is no spirit to serve in the public service — and for very similar reasons. The public service is governed by thousands of intricate regulations that give them every excuse to do nothing when something needs to be done and sinister, perverse opportunities to do things when they should not be done.

In closing this chapter, I will return briefly to the idea that communism is more a tool of the mega rich and powerful than a benevolent hand to lift up the poor and downtrodden.

Very few understand that communism has always been supported by some of the world's wealthiest people. The horrific regime that the Bolsheviks set up in Russia when they murdered the Czar and his family was funded by one of the world's wealthiest Jewish businessmen, Jacob Schiff (head of the Kuhn, Loeb and Company banking giant) to the tune of a gift of at least $2 billion in modern terms. Jacob Schiff also arranged loans in 1904 and 1905 to the Japanese that enabled them to defeat the Russians in the eastern war of that time, seriously weakening the Russian empire.

That largely Jewish led Bolshevik regime started a series of events that gave them immense power and the regime ended up killing tens of millions of innocent Russian people between 1918 and 1959 — possibly as many as 60 million people or 1.5 million per year. In truth however, the majority were probably killed in the first few bloodbath years.

The Bolshevik Politburo and controlled people with the most appalling of brutality, fear tactics and long-term starvation. These appalling strategies were designed to weaken the population physically and to suppress the egos of individuals within it.

This was the real holocaust of the twentieth century — enormously worse in sheer numbers and sheer horror than anything ever perpetrated on the European Jews during WW2 with around ten times the number of people believed to have been killed — and I will present this matter in greater detail in my epilogue to this book, The Bolshevik Threat.

Chapter 10 — The Concept of Anavah

You have heard it said that words are powerful and they are but I'd like to explore just how powerful they really are and why, not to mention what this might mean for us.

So just what do they do for us? Fundamentally, we do just two things in life. We perceive and we express and words facilitate both of these fundamentals. Just as we take in breath and exhale it, we take in what we experience, process it and express something in response to it that can either be described in words or actually conveyed by words.

Words help us define what we see and experience and thereby help us both to fully perceive and remember these things. They allow us to express what we think and feel about what we have seen and experienced. They also allow us to see and acknowledge what we desire and help us plan what we will do to achieve our needs and desires. Words are almost everything. They are used to guide and instruct us, to store knowledge, to entertain us and to facilitate healthy interaction between us. We literally build our world on words.

When we think in words instead of in images we can utilize verbal structures and concepts as tools that facilitate our response to experiences. We can apply these verbal engines to what we do and thereby create more pleasing and constructive outcomes.

So, we as individuals get a great deal out of using words but how do they affect us when they are used on us, to influence or control us? The truth is, words can be used both to liberate and to control.

I have found it fascinating to study the Christian Bible (so much so that I've written another book about it — The True Message of Jesus) because it was for so long the only written source of information and inspiration for many people. Many of its passages are purely allegorical and therefore open to broad interpretation but some very influential words have actually been changed — mistranslated or deliberately corrupted who can know?

Given the sordid, divided and violent history of the Christian Church and its immense power over the years, is it likely that the Bible would have been both used as an instrument of control and altered to facilitate that?

On reflection, I believe that few would conclude otherwise.

After all, the Roman Catholic Church forbade the translation of the Bible into the vernacular languages of the churchgoers for as long as it could. Translators were excommunicated and punished.

John Wycliffe translated the Bible into English in 1383 and his bones were later burned as the bones of a heretic. German and Spanish translations were burned and even as late as 1747, people were hanged for their involvement in 'Bible movements' as was Jakob Schmidlin of Switzerland. Even today, Canon 825 forbids the translation of sacred scriptures unless the Apostolic See approves them.

Certainly, religious authorities had an interest in using anything at their disposal to exert control over people and the Bible, as the supposed Word of God, had to say what was convenient and useful to them.

One of the most influential books in the Bible has always been the gospel of Matthew. It is the first book in the new testament and gives a clear account of Jesus's life with particular attention, three chapters, allocated to his most important instructions to his disciples in The Sermon on the Mount.

Of these verses, the so-called beatitudes are the most significant and of them, the one that offers the most specific instruction about how to behave along with the most tangible of rewards is 'the meek shall inherit the earth'. It always stood out in my mind and influenced me enormously for a long time.

I believe, in many ways, I became something of a doormat for others because of this statement of Jesus — a little amusing perhaps given that my given name was Matthew or Matt.

Did I harken to the other beatitudes? Not as much. In order, they promise (1) the kingdom of heaven (2) being comforted (4) being filled (5) obtaining mercy (6) seeing God (7) being called a child of God (8) and again the kingdom of heaven.

If Jesus says we will have the kingdom of heaven, is this not what all the worthy shall experience? The church tells us that all we have to do to get there is accept Jesus as our saviour. Most of us already receive comfort and are filled or fulfilled in all the ways we could reasonably expect. Most of us receive mercy and can expect to receive the mercy of God because we often show mercy to others in need.

Seeing God is frankly unimaginable and possibly frightening — even deadly if you believe the Old Testament. Finally, being called a child of god seems distinctly unremarkable given that is what we are generally called by the church anyway.

Yes, the only one of the beatitudes that has any tangible reward and requires us to modify our behaviour in any real, achievable fashion is the third of the eight, supposedly advising meekness. Three others talk about conscious approaches to behaviour that are of a very general nature. They honour mercy, hungering and thirsting after righteousness and being pure in spirit.

So, if we are to take Jesus' most spiritual and honoured set of instructions to heart, we should be merciful, meek, seek righteousness in what we do and try to be pure in spirit. Mercy is a given. There's nothing hidden or mysterious in that. Seeking righteousness is also fairly clear. Be honest. Be moral. Be caring. Being pure in spirit is more difficult. Who would really know what to do to achieve that, other than in doing all the other things that we're advised to?

So, the only tangible goal we can expect to achieve, inheriting the earth, we can achieve by doing something that we can relatively easily understand.

Being meek.

I think that like many believers, when I first encountered these scriptures, I didn't stop to properly analyse them and was left with a deep conflict in my soul. On one hand, the idea just seemed wrong without my realizing exactly why — yet at some level or other I also ended up thinking that I had a moral duty to be meek and forbearing, that I should let others have the first place all the time and that I shouldn't think my own priorities counted for anything, ever!

How futile such an attitude is, given that if everyone felt the same way, there would be absolute chaos? Can you imagine a situation where everyone was tripping over each other to do everything last, to get the least, to be the least noticed? Very Monty Python.

Well, for the poor and the humble, maybe it does seem to make sense. Why would they not take a tilt at it if they had a chance at inheriting the earth once paradise was established and eternal life set in place, just by doing things pretty much as they were already?

Ha!

In reality, meekness as most of us know it is absurd. We all deserve our share and should behave normally to try and get it.

And if we were to inherit the earth, surely that would mean that we were leaders beneath God, right? I mean, if you inherit something, you own it and if you own it, you get to call the shots with it, don't you? Are the meek going to do that? Are they even going to know how to do it given how little practise they will have given it in the rough and tumble of this existence?

Clearly, something is amiss and when you take a long, close look at the original Hebrew word that was translated into meek, anavah, you really have to begin to wonder. Others have, too.

Modern Bible authorities have looked at it in recent times and lo, they find that it was mistranslated! A new translation published in November 2013 says that the mild-tempered shall inherit the earth. Oh, and my, isn't that just so different? Isn't that really just another way of saying pretty much the same thing? And aren't most people mild-tempered? So, lots of normal average people are going to be the ones inheriting earth?

Given the chaotic nonsense you would get from everyone trying to be meek, maybe this mild-tempered thing might go some way towards obviating it but it still fails to hit the mark in all sorts of ways.

I mean, Jesus advocated anavah in his most famous sermon and when people advise doing something it's because it has worked for them, right? Moses, also, was said to be the most anavah person in religious history. Was he meek or even mild-tempered? Was Jesus?

I don't think so. This mild-tempered thing just does not sit right. It definitely seems at odds with the likes of Moses and Jesus and appears to be one of those concepts that has come to be accepted as true simply by consensus and weight of numbers rather than by deep enquiry and logical deduction.

Moses had to confront one of the world's most powerful rulers and defy him. And was Jesus mild tempered? No, he did not just confront the money lenders in the temple but he physically threw them out!

He also said that he did not come to bring peace but a sword and told us that if our parents or our children did not love him then we should give them up because they were unworthy. Those are not the words of a meek or mild man. They are more the words of a charismatic leader who demands loyalty.

Jennifer Ross in the website 'Torah Class' writes:
'These are days for those who are anav to be ever diligent and ever discerning so that we can stand against deceit or doubt.'

She extrapolates the word from how it was used with respect to Jesus and Moses to mean 'what god wants you to be' — and she says that these two much admired biblical figures are portrayed as men who are very much in tune with the concept of anav.

Without doubt, in other words, both were learned, considerate men, trying their hardest to understand and be at one with god's intent. Both were intelligent and aware, and were keen to foster a constructive, interactive learning relationship. Both also had great strength and owned the need for vigilance and diligence.

This is much closer to the mark.

So, if we can be reasonably sure that there was a big mistranslation in the first place, maybe we would be just a little gullible to accept the analysis of modern religious authorities. Maybe we should look a little further, dig a little deeper. When we look online at what various Jewish writers say about anavah, it is less about being meek or mild tempered than about having eyes to see, vigilance and diligence.

Yes, there are some articles on the internet, including some written by Jews, that speak of how the Hebrew word 'anavah' (a quality or state of mind in this form as opposed to 'anav' which is a person with this state of mind) contains conceptual elements typically associated with the mild character qualities sometimes found in men of learning — so I'll spend a little time trying to get to the heart of this and see if it really bears any weight.

The mildness or gentleness might have its source in the image of 'faithful servant' currently associated with the second letter 'nun' and linked with Moses through the symbology of an eel, which of course is a kind of fish, a symbol that is favoured in biblical culture.

Curious that. Why an eel and not a normal fish? Maybe it was what allowed them to facilitate the change of the original Egyptian symbology of the letter 'nun' from 'snake' to 'faithful servant'. An eel is like a snake and an eel is a kind of fish, which is linked with Moses because he was found as a baby in a river.

Apparently, Moses was a faithful servant to God but in doing God's work he was neither mild nor gentle, especially considering his attitude to Midianite women and children and to his violent, cruel statutes and judgements in Deuteronomy.

Even if we accept this idea of anavah being mild-tempered and assume that some learned people or some people initially involved in the process of learning can sometimes seem mild of manner, there have also been many others who were not mild tempered at all.

The greater, more significant historical elements of understanding this word in the context of Jesus and Moses being the epitome of anavah make the idea of it being mild-tempered simply too big a stretch. Anavah seems to be a question of having great personal spirit and spirit drives people to learn, to be aware and to enthuse over life; not to be mild.

In discussion with a learned Christian man of Jewish background back around 2008, I stated that I did not like the concept of religion advising people to be meek and he began to look at the source words.

After some time researching, he admitted that meek was a flawed translation and that there were implications of both learning and mildness associated with sheep and with the shepherds in the concept of anavah and that these implications might have relevance to the sort of attitude that is required for learning — a mild openness and willingness to learn symbolized by the image of an unwritten page.

Most people think of sheep as mild, gentle and willing to follow but if you've ever actually handled them, you'll know that they are not mild or gentle at all. They butt and they charge and bite. They run hard and dodge with great effectiveness so they can in fact be very difficult to control.

So, on one hand, the flock might be led and protected by the shepherd but on the other, they do not appear to give up their independence or self-will in any relevant way. Accordingly, the human flock should not manifest a blind acceptance and obedience without question.

At the very least, one must observe that there seems to be persistent debate about the concept of anavah, that no adequate consensus has been achieved and that the meaning is not completely clear.

In this context of doubt, there is in fact much more of interest to explore. Indeed, we have not even begun to scratch the surface.

Firstly, Hebrew is a very idiomatic language with subtleties and depths of meaning that go back into the mists of time. The words are made up from letters that are based on images, like the Egyptian hieroglyphs, so in a way the letters are in fact words in themselves. Apparently, many come from Egyptian.

Translation can be a very subjective thing at the best of times, especially when dealing with old languages and texts that were written in ancient times but this becomes more so when the root images of these words have been manipulated and become confused over time. Newer, flawed, interpretations of these root images can evolve out of a process akin to 'Chinese Whispers' or by political will, and this, on the evidence available, seems to have been what happened with 'anavah'. (anav-ness)

I am leading up, here, to the rational argument for a new alternate translation of the word but it would seem appropriate to preface it with a historical observation to place these deliberations in context.

Jesus would likely have been speaking in Aramaic to the crowds on Mount Erebus when he gave them the beatitudes and used this word. Even if his words were later translated into Koine Greek, his choice of words would have been shaped by his understanding of Aramaic and Hebrew. His use of the word 'anav' would certainly have had a particularly ancient foundation of understanding because he was quoting from Psalm 37, estimated to be written about 1000 BC.

Many students of the bible forget that context and seem to remain unaware that this usage from 1000 BC is not long after the first known use of Hebrew, around 1200 BC. Word usage at this time would probably involve meaning more closely related to the original images that were the source concepts of the letters probably from the Egyptian language.

So where do we look to find these source images? Without being an expert in ancient languages, there is really only one easily accessible solution — the internet. It readily provided me with a list of the main letters of the Hebrew alphabet along with comments about their likely origins. With this sort of information, it becomes possible to extrapolate a plausible original meaning.

So, let's construe anavah.

As I looked at the internet entries for these four letters I quickly saw a string of ancient concepts that spoke very loudly and clearly to me. Anavah comprises ayin (eyes to look and see), nun (snake), vaw, (mace) and he (an informal word for god, which used as a suffix implies moving towards him).

Sure, the 'nun' also now has associations with the faithful servant or very loosely with the feminine and technically in Hebrew the 'vaw' now means hook instead of the source Egyptian mace but I'll return to these things a little later to resolve the apparent differences.

I don't know about you but when I see eyes to see, snake, mace and moving closer to god, the message seems pretty clear. Have the awareness and vigilance to see potential dangers like snakes (reviled in the bible) and have the diligence to take a mace to them when you do. If you do so, you will be suitably rewarded by having a closer relationship with god.

So, from the most ancient word roots, anavah can be sensibly construed not to mean meekness or humility but awareness, vigilance and diligence or in more detailed terms 'something like: You will lead and be closer to god if you are willing to see and be vigilant about your surroundings while having the diligence to act strongly on your perception of the dangers'.

In other words, do not accept the will and opinions of others but act independently by using your god given skills and abilities. Thus, the perceptive, vigilant and the diligent will be able to build a relationship with god and find favour with him.

Do many have this ability to truly be their own man? The creative team of The West Wing, for one, believed this to be a rare thing. President Bartlett was intended to be the epitome of this rare character form and his senior staff were fiercely loyal to him because he was that most admirable thing — his own man.

This new meaning of the ancient pictographic letters, cobbled together out of ancient sources though it may be may be, is in accord both with the character of Moses, said, as previously mentioned, to be the most anav man in history, and with Jesus, who espoused the concept of anav and promoted it.

If we suspect mistranslation and or perversion of meaning in words over time, the fact is we can only do what I have done with this word and test the new hypothesis against the clearest character examples we have of these qualities.

Moses saw the danger to his people of continuing to be dominated and exploited any longer, took a whopping great hammer to the Egyptian pharaoh and his people — especially with respect to their first-born males — and in the process became closer to understanding and expressing God's will.

Jesus was a less obvious example of this emphatic sort of behaviour, despite his berating the money changers and literally throwing them out of the temple but he does typically display a thorough understanding of the need to see through the fog, perceive the dangers and act to avert them — as with his advice in Matthew 7:15 about deceivers or false prophets.

Are you going to reveal deceivers and expose false prophets by being meek?

So, this new hypothesis of anavah having a lost meaning closer to awareness and vigilance is supported by what we know of the character or great biblical figures — but is it also meaningful? Does it serve? Does it stand the ahah test, wherein we think, OMG, is this really something that we should be doing? Is it in fact what a just and reasonable God would wish us to be doing?

Jewish writers on the internet, like Rabbi David Jaffe, resolve the anomaly of anavah meaning humility or meekness and Moses being the most anavah man ever by attempting to create ever more complex definitions of humility, stating that it is more about healthy self-esteem (akin to my concept of moderated ego) and balance than about self-abasement. He says it is about taking up the appropriate amount of space in any context and once accepting a role, devoting oneself to it to the best of one's abilities.

This is a big stretch but it is still not truly Moses, or Jesus. Nor have Christians historically been encouraged to be meek in anything other than a completely subservient way.

Given that God rarely protects us directly, in the light of these examples of great and powerful figures like Moses and Jesus being anav men, we must presume that the divine creator wishes us to see clearly, perceive the dangers and find the strength to conquer them.

It would be very fitting that the most willing to do this — the very few — would inherit the earth. So, then let's go back to the issue of inheritance.

If you inherit something, you are its owner. With it, you take a leading role. The idea of inheriting the earth indicates the gift of a special role other than mere survival or existence within that framework. By demonstrating leadership qualities, you get that leadership.

So, this new concept of anavah, espousing enhanced perception, diligence and vigilance begins to make good sense on a number of levels and is close enough to more recent extrapolations of it by Jewish writers — but we still have to resolve the variant Hebrew letter meanings that vary so much between their possible ancient sources and those currently accepted in particular the key word 'vav' or 'vaw', which seems to be the main stumbling block in this interpretation of 'anav'.

These Hebrew 'vav' hooks are ceremonial silver fittings supposed to be attached to the stakes used to support the protective tent wall around the ark of the covenant and it is said that they symbolically connect heaven with earth.

Yet the letter symbol for 'vav' has a prior link with the Egyptian hieroglyph that meant mace and it is not unreasonable to ask why the meaning of this symbol might have changed.

I mean it's not drawing such a long bow to acknowledge the possibility that there could be an ancient, now hidden second meaning in such an idiomatically diverse language as Hebrew.

Addressing the most ancient symbolism then, a mace is a powerful, warlike hammer and a weapon worthy of expressing divine power. Thor had one that characterized his power.

Reputedly, the ancient Hebrew god acted at times with unmitigated power and wrath upon those of his people who transgressed his will, and this divine wrath could very well be seen as characterizing his interaction and connection with humanity.

If so, the people of that ancient time could hardly have missed the connection and might well have symbolized the key tool of his wrath as a quintessential link between heaven and earth.

Kick the dog and he becomes loyal to you. God hits the Hebrew (or his enemies) with a mace and the Hebrew is reminded of the strength and importance of god.

An anonymous writer on the 'bestirrednotshaken' website supports this view in stating that anavah is strongly associated with the fear of the Lord and quoting these passages to demonstrate it:

- "The fear of the Lord is the instruction of wisdom, and before honor is humility" (Prov. 15:33)

- "Before destruction the heart of a man is haughty, and before honor is humility" (Prov. 18:12)

Yet given the invidious nature of the ancient images of divine wrath and punishment linking heaven and earth — images that imply the somewhat embarrassing need for punishment, it would be no wonder if, over time, successive generations of priests wished to substitute a more friendly, neutral image in its place.

So, we get a change and if we look carefully at the nature of the change it tells us a lot. I mean, really, a ceremonial hook as a link between heaven and earth? It is very random given that the humble hook is not even directly connected with the ark. One can imagine a committee deciding on just such a thing, likely because it was meaningless and offensive to no one.

Some say that the concept of anavah was and still is the keystone of Hebrew behavioural culture; the conduct asked of man by god himself. Yet the original word held elements that would have been uncomfortable to priests and laity alike, if not properly understood. For one thing, nun means snake or eel in Aramaic and the Hebrew word for snake begins with nun. The snake, certainly is not adored in this culture.

My interpretation of those ancient symbolic letters is a positive one construing the overall meaning to be an instruction from god to be wary of the dangers in life and to work at enhancing your perception so that you can be aware of them and deal with them efficiently.

What if some generation of Hebrew leaders or other instead interpreted it as something like 'anyone who has the eyes to see will understand that God punishes snake-like people with wrath and suffering?

We all experience suffering in this world in ways that might well be seen as the wrath of god. Every man experiences misfortune at times and if this vital, central religious concept of the mace gave early priests any cause to doubt themselves or have doubt cast upon them — any cause for embarrassment, they would have been anxious to modify the meaning of the letter either immediately or over time.

So, at the very least, the reviled snake might not have been welcome in the limited Hebrew alphabet and the priests might well have been inspired to alter the meaning of 'nun' to eel instead, which it now is in Aramaic.

An eel is a kind of fish and Moses himself was known as a fish because he was retrieved from the waters of the Nile as a babe. Most salubrious indeed to have this important letter in this vitally important word associated instead with god's most loyal, faithful servant.

The same thing might very well apply to another divergent meaning of 'nun'. Nun as an abbreviation can stand for 'neqeveh' which means feminine. There is in the Hebrew creation mythology a uniquely significant relationship between the serpent and the feminine. Eve, in the story of the fruit of the Tree of Knowledge of Good and Evil was clearly quite familiar with the serpent and happily received guidance from it. She must have considered herself closely aligned with it to act on its advice in direct defiance of god.

Ancient Hebrew scholars would of course have been completely aware of this relationship and some would no doubt have felt great satisfaction in unifying the snake and the feminine in the concept of 'nun' at least in one of the various idioms of the word. Many of them would have found it most apt that the warning about the dangers that men should 'have eyes to see' should specifically involve the feminine.

I'm not sure about ancient Hebrew culture but I do know that the later Christian culture advocated beating women once a week in a physically non-damaging way both to keep them emotionally balanced and to keep them out of trouble.

The mace used in this context would be an approximation only. In the necessarily limited image base of an idiomatic, pictographic language like ancient Hebrew, a mace is not so very different to a stick or a whip, with which an ancient tribesman might be expected to beat a wife or daughter. It is simply a tool of force or weapon and a whip or lash or belt is also a sort of weapon.

Hence maybe there was another meaning something like 'have the eyes to see the dangers of women and punish them to keep them closer to the principles of behaviour pleasing to god.

Yet in all truth, my favoured meaning of perception, vigilance and diligence already encompasses dealing with any possible danger so it need not be as specific as 'watch your woman'.

Even so, the same priests who objected to the presence of the snake in their holy alphabet would likely have been equally reluctant to allow the continued association of the feminine with it, if only because of woman's association with the serpent.

All this ancient word analysis is admittedly very speculative but since this interpretation of the word 'anavah' fits so well with the characters of those Biblical figures who even modern Jewish writers regard as the most 'anav' in history, it seems justifiable to look for such lost or obscured connections.

Where an ancient and obscured body of knowledge has apparent anomalies, we must speculate and these speculations are all we have. Therefore, they must have profound consequences for the way we understand any associated knowledge.

Words can have secondary meanings of course, especially in ancient Hebrew, and a further construction of the word 'anavah' as willing to learn or teachable is supported to some extent by its use in Psalm 25.9 and the book of Zephaniah (2 III) in the Old Testament.

Of course, this meaning does also tie in with my new one because being willing to learn is in accord with enhanced perception. In this sense, receptive would be the most apt translation and maybe that is where the link with the feminine comes in.

The psalm says "The meek will he guide in judgement: and the meek will he teach his ways". Surely this would make perfect sense if we were to translate the phrase as 'The vigilant and the curious to know (receptive) will he guide in judgement'. And 'the curious to know will he teach his ways'. If any of you have ever tried to teach anyone something, you will know how satisfying and rewarding it is when they are truly curious and willing to learn. Conversely, it is very difficult to teach someone who does not want to know.

Zephaniah also says "seek righteousness, seek humility" and later "but I will leave within you the meek and humble ... who will do no wrong ... speak no lies".

Zephaniah was probably written no earlier than 640 BC, which is not nearly as old as Psalm 37. Possibly by then even, the meaning of anavah had begun to change or maybe the humble was added to the meek in Christian translations of these texts much later.

But why would you do no wrong and speak no lies? Because you know what is right from having a spirit of vigilance and having the eyes to see, are of course willing to learn.

In any case, if we substitute receptive, along with perceptive, vigilant and diligent, for meek (and humble), these quotes actually make much more sense.

The receptive he shall guide in judgment and the receptive will he teach his ways. I will leave within you the vigilant and the diligent who will do no wrong ... speak no lies.

Both of these quotes considered together indicate that god will guide us in our learning of the truth but that we must first seek to find it; righteousness and the truth. This is in perfect accord with the proposed meaning of anavah as awareness, vigilance and diligence.

So, a mild temper might make a person more open and willing to learn and be aware — a concept that could effectively be represented in the image of the unwritten page that seems to have become associated at least a little with anavah — but it would hardly guarantee it.

Moreover, the concept of the unwritten page is overly simplistic when considering the best sort of learning processes in a real-life context, assuming the need for compliance when in fact the independently individual qualities of perceptiveness, challenge and diligence are required.

The key focus for properly understanding the process of teaching here is knowing that the page will always, to some extent, be partially written on already and that valuable new concepts can be found when a teacher is willing to trace the path through what the student or child already knows.

Expecting children to be meek, mild and compliant in the learning process effectively dictates that teachers would ignore what is already written on their page. Can anyone truly imagine a mild and compliant child raising his hand and challenging the tall, imposing teacher over something he, the child, already knows?

You are only truly teachable if you are ready to learn — keen, curious and diligent rather than meek, mild and compliant.

And you can only be a good teacher when you are willing both to continue to learn and to find out just what your student already knows.

Bah, to the unwritten page!

Crucially, such subtle adventures in learning contribute very effectively to teachers continuing to learn. The ones who have the 'eyes to see', discovering new aspects of concepts hidden amongst what the child already knows, will be the best teachers. And this worthy execution of the learning/teaching process is crucially important because it can reveal new things and thereby increase the sum total of human understanding.

The unwritten page is, therefore, more an undiscovered path through much that is already written, and in the light of earlier conclusions, it is reasonable to conclude that the concept of 'anavah' must involve a willingness to seek insight, to see the lay of the land and to act to protect yourself — rather than simple meekness or mild temperedness.

So, if meek is useless bull then what is its opposite? Ego? Spirit? Do they in fact have value?

Nearly everyone will have heard that Jesus said 'The meek shall inherit the earth' and this has influenced vast numbers to behave in a meek fashion, accepting slavery and oppression to serve predators who were in many instances inferior to themselves.

Meekness serves no constructive purpose whereas ego, properly moderated, has a number of very important functions. Some people with strong egos are purely self-seeking egomaniacs with no loyalties to anything but themselves but in most cases, this is not so. Many strong individuals create great things and lead fulfilling lives inspired by the desires of a healthy ego.

Governments and large organizations tend to promote ego suppressing concepts like service to God, service to the state and general self-sacrifice because it serves the goals of the individuals running them. God, my friends, is in no special need of your service and if the state wants it, it should damn well pay for it and receive it gratefully on your terms.

What a tragedy it is to misunderstand God when he would clearly expect us to learn, grow and adapt with the use of the free will that he gave us. To use the intellect properly invokes worthy pride rather than humility and tends to build a sense of individual responsibility rather than meekness and conformism.

Truly understanding the concept of anavah will change peoples' lives. They will be duped less by the powers of the world, will be happier, healthier, more intelligent and much closer to the existence that God intends for them.

As more people understand this crucial, fundamental truth, the balance of power in the world will be drawn away from those who have been corrupted by evil and placed more in the hands of the worthy. We will indeed inherit the earth.

It's a big thing.

Chapter 11 — Anavah and The Value of Emotions (4)

In the light of these insights about meekness, we should also more carefully examine our cultural perception of the concept of ego.

Since 'anavah' came over time to have an association with mildness, humbleness, learning and children, the closest the Greeks could come to translating it was to use their word 'praus', (prah-ooce) which some say means humble, forbearing and meek. Others say it has its roots in horse management, symbolizing the orderly power held in reserve symbolized by a well-trained mount — a matter of discipline.

The adoption of 'praus' may have been no more than a cultural misunderstanding on their part but the strange blurring of the concept could also have reflected conscious intent to promote the subjection of people that the more martial style of leadership prevalent in Roman and some Greek cultures with which they would be more comfortable.

Yet the word 'praus' is not really all that significant for our purposes because 'anav' is the word Jesus would have used when speaking to his audience on the mount.

Anavah is the thing to focus on, given that the cultural obsession with meek is also consistent with the unhealthy and unjust imbalance of power in the clergy and laity dichotomy typically associated with organized, institutionalized religion throughout European history since the takeover of Christianity.

The clergy has most often sought to suppress ego and clearly the only cogent reasons for encouraging the suppression of ego are ones that serve total control. Just watch all those religious leaders use their ego to suppress ego in their followers. It suits the power-hungry very well to have their flocks believe ego has no place since suppressing it also supresses individual thought and responsibility.

The Catholic Church, for instance, was so little interested in informing its flock, hardly in keeping with the complex and subtle meaning of the Hebrew word 'anav', that for many centuries it forbade them to read the Bible at all and made it difficult to do so by banning translation into any language other than Latin.

In any case, a philosophy of fluid interaction with the world would say, instead, that the ego, along with everything else, has its place. Yet it has been the policy of religions to denigrate ego and it would be ingenuous to believe that it had nothing to do with the fact that ego is the essence of individual strength.

For better or worse, there is strong evidence to suggest that the ego is extremely resilient and adaptable. It seems reasonable to ask, then, why should anyone even contemplate eliminating it? In a modern world of science and reason, it makes more sense to recognize that it might be there for very good reasons.

If the path to mental clarity is to be trod, a more effective understanding of ego must be reached. Trying to expunge or suppress it might ultimately prove to be no better than psychological, emotional self-mutilation. Plainly, there are at least two views on the matter and if the issue is to be resolved, it will be necessary to explore them thoroughly.

Ego can be seen as a contributing element to human personality or it can be regarded as a rampant monster suitable only to be repressed and negated in every way until, supposedly, it utterly disappears.

If ego had to be defined simply as the uncontrolled drive to achieve the most sensual satisfaction in the shortest possible time, it probably would be worth negating. Such a view is, however, overly simplistic and does not recognize or acknowledge that ego can be constructively modified.

Plainly, the first impulses of the ego should be examined before giving expression to them. In most cases, these impulses will not need intervention but when conscious appraisal determines the potential for trouble in a course of action, an alternate way for the ego to be satisfied should be found and expressed.

So, we can effectively accommodate ego — but does it have a constructive purpose that we cannot safely do without? Considering the above process of modifying impulses, it might in fact be our first stage perceptual filter, establishing initial focus on what the mind can and should experience.

In fact, it would hardly be surprising if ego was primarily intended for this purpose since most of what people notice, out of the vast sum of what could be seen, is what they wish or expect to see.

Ego and emotion are strongly linked in human experience and this attracts greater significance if you believe, as I do, that great and unfettered emotional experiences, linked as they are through dreaming to the astral realm, might actually be key building blocks that will contribute to shaping our future eternal beings.

Even if that is not the case, it cannot be denied that emotions are an enormously important and rewarding part of life and that they may be the fuel for the best possible experience of our ongoing existence.

It has long been of great interest for me to note that even when memory impaired people fail to remember the details of past events, environmental stimuli can trigger emotional experiences associated with those events and restore the memory, which indicates that something other than physical biochemical memory is at play.

As seen in Alzheimer's cases, large parts of the brain are destroyed and physical memories have been entirely deleted yet key emotional triggers can be used to stimulate awareness and recollection of memories. It is like these people are living in a dream and the filter of the brain that organizes rational things like time has been eroded away but even without that, the soul recalls powerful experiences with these emotional triggers.

So, what is doing the remembering? If you believe in an afterlife of any kind, something immaterial has to preserve elements of awareness and identity, and what would be more important to preserve in the astral sphere than the powerful, revealing and life changing emotional events that contribute so much to our identity?

Is it not also significant that our best and most memorable dream experiences, also clearly linked to the astral plane, are frequently imbued with similar vivid emotional elements? Vivre, live, vivid? Wasn't this also the essence of spirit?

In any non-material state of existence, we have to assume that experience of existence would be much like what it is when we have the clearest, most beautiful and lucid dreams. So, when we generate and feel these great and powerful emotional experiences, we may well be forging vital (there's that prefix again) elements of our future super-material or non-physical existence.

In that high goal, ego may well be our principal guide and if that job is to be done properly the ego's priorities will need to be projected effectively into the state of play. This clearly does not mean letting it run rampant with irresponsible actions but it might well mean letting it guide the general direction of our experience.

The latter constructive role is possible because vigilant, diligent intellect is there to guide the ego to veto any truly unacceptable alternatives and to facilitate the best possible experience. With that guiding hand, many things can be safely experienced that might otherwise entail destructive and negative outcomes.

Based on experience, if ego is ignored or repressed, eventually its priorities will come to the fore anyway but given the increasing urgency of its demands, it would be more likely to ride roughshod over the intellect with grave consequences. If so, any resulting experience would be much less likely to happen in a safe and reasonable manner.

It would be unwise and wilfully ignorant to avoid acknowledging that the ego is a powerful thing but a careful thinker will draw the distinction between an integrated ego and a rampant one.

An out of control ego will destructively attempt to fulfil its desires against all odds and in spite of all other reasonable considerations. In contrast, a well-integrated ego will defer to good judgment, allowing it to provide reasonable goals as well as a sense of direction and emotional satisfaction. This will contribute to a strong sense of identity, given that the proper use of intellect seems to reward the mind with positive emotions.

With so many choices to be made about what to pursue in life, it can only seem reasonable to suppose that there should be an aspect of personality geared towards prioritizing matters of interest. Few people can rationally justify what they find amusing or important. It is simply what they prefer and that is what ego allows them to do — determine basic priorities.

A clear, harmonious relationship between the emotional and the intellectual is therefore likely to be crucial for generating a positive adaptation to both life and the afterlife, and a generally favourable attitude towards emotional ego, consciously acknowledging its merits, completes the circle.

Who really knows how it works but it certainly helps us to maintain mood and balance in difficult circumstances to have some idea about how all the mysteries come together into a clear picture.

Chapter 12 — The Role of Intellect in Freedom

As I stated at the outset of this exploration of the future of human leadership, slavery has been a long enduring tradition throughout the world and if you want to avoid being a slave then you had better use your brain — use your brain to define yourself and what you choose to aim for in this life. You also need to use your brain to work out when you are being conned or misdirected.

In other words, you must have the 'eyes to see' — the will to see beyond the obvious.

Reason, the basis of all constructive learning, is the process that will get you through these many challenges but you cannot get the best results from reason unless you know very clearly how it works and for this reason specifying and discussing the basic process has to be an indispensable and integral part of the plan for our new constructive world.

High up on the list of concerns in this process is the need to discover and chip away at all those inherited and largely unfounded assumptions that lay like traps, or snakes to tread on, (bruising heals) in all our subconscious minds.

These are pieces of BS that are shared widely in a community yet which are largely unexamined and their sway is not in their truth so much as in the weight of numbers that unconsciously hold them to be so.

These unfounded assumptions make communal identity much more likely to be a pitfall and a source of weakness than a resource when it comes to building a better world or to enhancing consciousness, especially when society has long been sabotaged by the insanities of corrupted organized religion.

While not the easiest thing to do, discovering these self-defeating assumptions can be done relatively quickly and efficiently with the right tools. The most important of these tools is rational thought — in particular, where constructive results are required, zetetic questioning.

The beauty of this process of zetetics is its sheer simplicity. While a comprehensive understanding of the field of logical thought might be feasible for some, most people would find the full range of its formal rules very complex and tedious to learn. Given its complexity, it might even end up placing blinkers on eyes instead of allowing them to see.

Resolving issues effectively in everyday life requires something much more handy and user friendly and for that need there is nothing better than zetetics. It provides a simple yet effective method for exploring concepts and making good choices quickly and easily.

Given the importance of seeing things clearly in life, I'll cover zetetics in greater detail soon.

At the moment, things are not exactly as they should be. It seems clear that while many people have some sort of hazy definition of rational thought they do not actually know how to employ it or even exactly what it is. Most will have heard of it of course but to be able to use it effectively, they would have to have explored it and to have understood a specific definition.

This is a fundamental principle of consciousness. If you do not directly explore concepts yourself, you cannot fully understand them. When you are diligent and you do fully explore them, many liberating benefits come to light so your relationships with everything improve.

Solid improvement in the area of human thought requires the discovery and use of a specific method that can be easily understood and rapidly applied in the most challenging of circumstances.

Defining the most basic and important functions that the intellect has to perform in daily life can facilitate this adaptive process. By enhancing intellectual function, the 'observer' has 'eyes to see' or the power to see the world more reliably through the filter of the intellect, rather than solely through the raw perceptual capacity of the senses and the basest forms of emotion.

The observer perceives what seems important to him. Then, if he is diligent, he can analyse the situation to work out what is best to do in it and ultimately express his will through concerted, well-integrated actions. In the proper execution of this process, the mind employs the two primary aspects that work in concert with each other — thought and feeling.

Yes, they can work very well together but if they are to work effectively together and allow us to be decisive, they have to be balanced.

The goal of maximized consciousness can only be achieved if both mental polarities function alongside each other with smooth efficiency. Otherwise, perception will be muddied and obscured, analysis will be flawed and expression will be incoherent. One could say that with the latter mindset, the snake will get away unscathed and you will have a bruised heel.

Those who have become motivated to assess their own understanding of reasoning for the first time might well find their actual awareness of its rules is limited, vague and generalized. It is possible for a person to discover, after years of assuming they were rational adults, that their ability to think consciously and analytically was actually something of a mirage.

In view of the fact that everyone makes choices hundreds of times a day and it is how they make those choices that determines their overall wellbeing and success, it is truly chilling to think how much damage might have been caused by botched thinking that has coloured decisions.

When a person comes up with their own specific definition of rational thought, they might well conclude that they have been employing something like it all along when pushed to meet extraordinary challenges but that their command of it was limited and sporadic.

Many would have assumed up until then that they were in command of the faculty of reason and would have believed that simply because they had often heard the word used in conversations and understood it to be an important function of the human mind.

Such a misapprehension would be a major stumbling block to constructive self-development and therefore, feeling a little dismay and disbelief in facing the existence of such an oversight would be natural. Yet any such realization ought in the end to be cause for self-congratulation given the possibility of then addressing the deficiency, the lack of anavah, and initiating transformational change.

Rational analysis is a vital tool and it ought to be the cause of great pride and confidence to know that you have it truly at your command. Therefore, it is something worth double checking and in doing that I will offer a brief summation against which the reader's self-assessment might be measured.

For rational analysis to be done effectively, the individual need only have a simple, reliable definition that can translate into a method employable easily on the timescale of thought — in other words, almost instantly. If the process needs to be quick, it must be simple, which is the main benefit of zetetics, since it uses a very simple straightforward question and answer process to find the best solutions.

If you have achieved a clear definition of rational thought and frequently employ it, that is admirable but failing that, if you explore someone else's definition, fully comprehend the truth of it and adopt it consistently, it will also serve you well. Bear in mind that adopting someone else's definition certainly does not mean you cannot further refine it.

If you think you might not have got to the crux of reason yet, you might need to look at a few different definitions to break down the barrier.

One dictionary definition is "to reach conclusions from premises". Another is "to reach conclusions by connected thoughts" and a third is "to draw conclusions from facts". All are true but the tricky part is in choosing what facts to consider, in connecting your thoughts pertinently and reliably and in deciding what your premises will be.

The first step is to decide what basic purpose you wish to use reason for — discovering a truth or finding the best way to do something. In discovering truth, you would first state a premise which would stand as the foundation of your current belief. Then you would test it. With the second, you would specify the desired result — the final product. After that, the successive steps on the path to realizing that objective could be initiated relatively easily.

Although it is simple on the face of it, a number of fine-tuning issues should be considered. Sometimes there is little time to plan an effective set of steps to the desired objective and if you seem to be having a lot of difficulty in this part of the process, it might be because you have not established a sufficiently clear objective. If so, it will be next to impossible to build an effective strategy.

So, at the outset, considerable energy ought to be given to the formulation of a clear statement about your objective. With that, the steps by which the desired result might be effectively achieved can be much more easily identified and accurately specified. This then suggests a series of suitable actions for each step in reaching your desired objective.

Some goals require many steps and choices to achieve so at every step in the process, reason should dictate a generally appropriate step. In other words, a good reason should be evident as to why the step is appropriate. That is why this basic and most useful level of constructive thought is called reasoning.

Beyond that, a significant part of reasoning is finding the mental energy to go that one step further in finding an alternative at each step that is the best possible solution. Therefore consider at least three alternative solutions from which to choose at each step — one of the basic techniques of zetetics.

Making conscious choices is vital since if a choice that has public consequences turns out to be wrong, and they can sometimes despite our best efforts, the chooser's reputation can only be protected by presenting the reasoning process that led to the choice.

It is generally forgivable to make a mistake if an effort to apply rational thought was made even if it turned out to be flawed but if no rational process was employed, it is rightly seen as carelessness. That is irresponsible and therefore less forgivable. Personal integrity demands that people should be answerable or responsible for themselves and their actions.

Importance of the Six Fundamental Emotions (6)

Minds without ready access to rational thought tend to cause ongoing trouble, being far too easily swayed by unexamined impulses that may or may not have real emotions behind them. While we should not use reason to suppress the expression or consideration of emotion, we should not let emotions shape our outward actions without any inner debate.

Emotions are vitally important. They mediate our core desire from day to day and regulate our intellect. Emotions and intellect balance each other and one must not be weighed greater than the other. Emotions also have a significant influence over memory and may well shape our after-life experiences so it might be very important to experience the best of them despite the greatest challenges. Looking for the bright side of things will always help in this.

Suppression of emotion will lead to negative emotions, whereas, the willing experience of emotion will be rewarding no matter how difficult or scary the experience is initially.

Consciousness can never be automatic and given that most of us lead our lives on automatic most of the time, we become accustomed to letting our emotions lead the way in our outward expressions and reactions without proper reference to conscious rational thought. All we really need to do is properly experience emotions and consciously weigh what they tell us if they persist in being at odds with the intellect.

Letting emotions lead us automatically is clearly not ideal because it would be out of balance and a smooth synthesis of emotion and intellect is what we need.

Possible courses of action suggested by emotion other than those clearly suggested by rational thought should be considered if our intuition or our conscious act of emotional assessment tells us very strongly that what seems obvious might be wrong.

The fact is, under such circumstances, it could be possible that we are missing crucial pieces of information perhaps not yet available, so without these, the intellect cannot properly make a good decision.

If there was something important that you did not know, it would be near impossible to get the best from the situation intellectually, so acting from your emotional perception might serve, as long as you can stand back calmly and carefully observe how things unfold — ready to modify events as they unfold and more information becomes available.

Getting the best from this process depends like everything else on the proper understanding and awareness of the fundamentals.

The Six Core Emotions

We have covered the basics of intellect so now we need to explore emotions. The six fundamental emotions come in dualistic pairs. The first pair is love and hate or disgust. The second pair is peace or contentment and anger. The third is curiosity and ignorance. All of these amount to either acceptance or rejection. They are three basic dichotomies of acceptance and rejection that relate to the personal world of our inner being, the social world and the material world — the three main spheres we engage with during our lives in this world.

We need to define them in such basic terms because recognizing the source of the feelings we experience will help us to come to terms with them.

As you begin to see the possibilities opened up by the balance of clear rational thought with willingly experienced emotion, it will become obvious why so many poor decisions are made in society.

For one thing, since it is so much easier to conform than to be different, especially in the constant company of others, society is very subject to mental inertia, wherein emotions are suppressed and intellect is held in disrespect.

With such a strong tendency in this direction, social awareness needs to be actively reprogrammed to support the propagation of understanding about these basic mental processes. Everyone stands to benefit. More people would be able to contribute effectively and the quality of life would vastly improve.

If people do not have a healthy and conscious respect for balanced rational thought, they will not have faith in what it reveals. On the other hand, if they do have faith in balanced rational thought they will be diligent and seek to extend its capacity.

Another factor then comes into play. Rational thinking capacity can be greatly enhanced by employing well-established thought patterns to facilitate the best sorts of outcomes in a range of different situations. These mental structures are concepts — previously established structures of thought that apply, like principles, with equal suitability in a variety of circumstances.

Sophisticated concepts are tools of great power. The sense of reward in using them is easily as satisfying as that given by any more tangible tool but, in doing so, the seeker of a healthy identity also reinforces their pride in their ability to think rationally

The ensuing mental strength helps to ensure that the voice of ego does not manifest in an unruly way, and greatly facilitates making quick, reliable decisions in the heat of the moment.

I will provide five examples now of concepts that will demonstrate their power and significance.

*Appreciation of paradox. If something seems to be one way yet it does not make much sense that it is that way, awareness of the concept of paradox would suggest that your understanding of the matter could be further explored, until you see why it does make sense.

*Mutual need. The golden rule effortlessly guides you towards good conduct. Our first concern is quite naturally ourselves but reason dictates that we need to care about others because in the most basic terms, the mental and physical states of others, particularly those close to us, will always have a significant effect on us. Naturally many of us simply care, as well.

*Reverse psychology. Using it allows you more freedom to move in reacting to people when they may be constrained by expectations or relationship dynamics. This can be very revealing but it should never be used as a weapon unless using it on an enemy.

*Loose lips sink ships. The resolve to achieve desired goals is a form of power like stored water or electricity. Release it unnecessarily in idle gossip and you will rarely if ever achieve anything, even if the information does not leak out to someone who can actually undermine your enterprise.

*Knowledge is power. People often state this without knowing the full truth of it. Complete awareness of the structure or makeup of particular things will enable surprisingly agile manoeuvres. You can end up where you wish to be much more easily than you would have thought possible. Look at the detailed structure of things and ask what drives them.

Clear awareness of concepts overall will not only facilitate thought but memory as well, since recollection depends so much on coherency.

Discovery — personal, material and cultural — through smooth flowing integrated thought is a very real and appreciable pleasure. It can reveal welcome and satisfying solutions in all areas of day-to-day life and yield positive feelings as well.

Each time some piece of knowledge arcane or otherwise, is integrated into verbal form in the mind via a process of reasoning and the conceptual relationship between it and other things is revealed, the ego rewards the mind bio-chemically. Immediate pleasure can be found in the comprehension of something not previously known and in the knowledge that the mind can become increasingly adept at finding its way around this vast, complex and challenging universe.

Integration of knowledge via consistent reasoning can also lead to the development of more mysterious abilities. It is rewarding for instance to be able to acquire something simply by visualizing it. To know more than simply the name or appearance of something, and to know something of the structure and function of it as well, is to liberate a formidable power.

The more complete the visualization in all aspects of the object's nature, the more likely it will quickly and accurately come into your life, although it might arrive in an unexpected form — one even more pertinent and helpful than you might have foreseen. It might seem to some like it draws upon unearthly powers but in fact it works best through a calm appreciation of the divine.

It works because it is natural prayer in a form that the divine appreciates — not vague generalities repeated over and over again. This is the meaning of the scripture that advises us to seek god first and then everything else will be added unto you.

Such feats of the mind are playful and amusing but they are far from being frivolous. Quite apart from the emotional charge it can give, it can also help you get what you need and wish for more efficiently, thereby saving you from becoming overwhelmed by a typically large flood of material cares and concerns. Thus, it maximizes the time that can be devoted to a fuller appreciation of existence.

Every time a person cultivates their capacity for imagination through the synthesis of rational thought and emotion in everyday use, their sense of identity will grow stronger and better. This empowers the generative ability of both thought and prayer.

Seeking god in this world is seeking understanding of his creation so seeking focal points to concentrate upon is a great way to enhance both identity and a relationship with the divine.

The issues that you might explore can be surprisingly simple. What word should be used in a particular context, and are there deeper aspects to that word's meaning? How should something be done and what will be the ramifications of such actions? What is your current destination and how will it be reached? What is needed and how will it be got?

After all, what use is there in knowing how to use rational thought balanced with emotion if the ability is rarely employed? So, keep it simple and keep it up.

The Physical, Perceptual Plane (4)(c)

Without the sorts of challenges physical existence presents in terms of sheer survival, we would all long ago have slipped into sloth and terminal boredom, as with circumstances so often documented wherein people suddenly and unexpectedly receive or win large sums of money in lotteries, removing the normal factor of challenge from their lives.

This is the crucial significance of the physical/ perceptual plane of existence to which many religious leaders over time have attributed evil qualities. Yet it is a crucial catalyst for our spiritual growth and development. As such it should be respected and we should understand that there are vast fields of knowledge in this plane of existence which are enormously important. It contains much hidden meaning but also a balanced cradle within which the soul and the spirit can develop.

It's important to recognize how and why people view life negatively, given that peoples' motives and conduct are governed by what they believe. We can dodge a lot of bullets if we understand how these negatives attitudes come about.

For one thing, negative attitudes can come from long-standing existential boredom. If our circumstances are comfortable and we are not challenged by immediate survival issues, we can become bored and even anxious. Under these circumstances, active use of the intellect to find meaning and clarity is a positive response. We might also run a business or become politically involved yet if we are unable to find fulfilment in such things, we might become resentful and even destructive.

Such a state could be seen as being like getting stuck in quicksand. Improving material or economic circumstances can take away the fundamental need to respond to the basic challenges of existence but so too can attaining a state of emotional equilibrium through such things as meditation and self-analysis.

Yes, paradoxically, even such seemingly constructive things can be bad in excess, especially when we lack a strongly felt sense of purpose in our lives.

Equilibrium and meaning are the two fundamental axes of our reaction to life and like so many things they must be in balance.

On one hand, we want the balanced emotions that equilibrium offers but on the other hand if we have too much of it, the excitement and meaning in our life diminishes. The equilibrium becomes a smothering effect. A well-adjusted mind will seek both in equal measure. Once consistent equilibrium has been attained, seeking meaning becomes a more urgent priority.

The more fully emotional equilibrium can be attained, the more significant 'meaning' becomes, since it provides the most effective means to jolt the spirit out of any self-created stability that otherwise becomes stale, lifeless and boring.

So, this is one of the ways that zetetics can be applied very effectively — as a valuable balance tool. Making choices in life is not solely about consulting the intellect and rational principles. It is also very much about knowing what we truly desire, what we wish for and where we see ourselves in life both in physical and emotional terms.

We can very easily make perfectly reasonable decisions that are no good for us, that bore us, that do not work out well and give us no pleasure. Yet the intellect is always involved one way or another and the solution lies in finding ways to make decisions that are both reasonable and desirable.

Since we have intellect, we have to use it and can use it to avoid being driven by negative emotions and patterns of drama such as Eric Byrne elucidated in his book, 'The Games People Play' but we can also use it positively to make choices that will have the best of outcomes in our physical and emotional lives.

Zetetics

Everyone owes it to his or her development, and to the world in general, to know more about zetetics. Over the ages, knowledge of zetetics has been obscured by the destruction of libraries in ancient times but new insights inspired from the bones of what was left reveal that this key philosophy deserves much greater acclaim.

In the modern era, it has made a gradual comeback, partly because of Marcello Truzzi's adoption of the concept and his use of the word in the name of his sceptic's magazine, *Zetetic Scholar*. Yet the detail remained obscure.

More than ever in this complex and sophisticated world, we need a system of thought that will lift us out of the mud. An extensive knowledge of the formal rules of rational thought and logic would contribute greatly to the development of anyone's thought processes but as things stand, most would balk at the time and effort required to acquire such knowledge. Most would also find it difficult to apply in day-to-day life.

At a casual glance, the discipline of logic seems so complex and difficult that in our busy world, a want of enthusiasm for it is understandable. In the hectic 21st century, few feel that they can spare the time to explore any philosophy, let alone a complex one.

Yet the difficulties that we might encounter in learning to think clearly and systematically by no means dispense with the great need to do so.

With such great need to perform well hanging over us, we should jump at the answer and the answer is zetetics.

So, what is zetetics?

The short answer is, 'to proceed by enquiry', to proceed by asking questions either in the discovery of truth or in the determination of the best course of action, both of which can yield great rewards. This light but direct description of a powerful ancient philosophy was until recently all that was left of it because of the destruction of the ancient library at Alexandria.

While the instruction 'to proceed by enquiry' might seem patently obvious, there's a lot more to it than first meets the eye. Clearly, any logical process like zetetics demands the specification of a process used in its execution.

Unfortunately for humanity, the finer details of zetetics were lost long ago, perhaps one of those seemingly obvious elements that have been taken for granted yet that Gestalt would have us examine more carefully. Zetetics' earliest known proponent was Pyrrho but he never wrote anything about it and because the works of his student, Timon, have mostly been lost, only the sketchiest outline remains.

Yet thought clarity was clearly Pyrrho's goal and exploring the means to facilitate it within the sole simple context of suspending final judgment and 'proceeding by enquiry' allows rediscovery relatively easily and leads rapidly to some unexpected and exciting insights.

By means of basic logical deduction, zetetics demands the specification of a process in the execution of questioning that would help people, explore concepts and make good choices in matters of importance.

We already know that one of the most crucial aspects of reasoning is questioning but the process of questioning within the sphere of reasoning has not really been codified and zetetics is a great headline concept under which this can be done.

With the establishment of a few key elements zetetics can give us a surer stance in the modern maelstrom of existence. The key considerations in any process of questioning are that you should establish your goal and thereby create a premise. When you question something, you should always make sure you answer the question rather than simply doubting the validity of something because it is under question. Lastly, you should always make sure to consider multiple viable alternative answers to each question asked.

It is vital to cultivate an acute awareness that the act of questioning is more than simply raising doubt over something. I emphasize this because this business of simply doubting something because a query has been raised over it is a strong negative element in our culture. People do it all the time and it manifests some of its greatest harm in the act of mudslinging.

Many people do stall their thinking processes at the point where doubt is raised over something and never properly resolve the doubt. No doubt, the reasons for this are cultural or environmental factors rather than any innate, intellectual deficiency in reasoning capacity.

In any case, when people do fail to resolve any matter about which they are thinking, they typically move on in the same fashion only to treat the next matter in equally shallow terms.

In truth, this deficiency of thinking means that people can grind to a halt by inadequate questioning rather than 'proceeding by enquiry' through employing it properly, as the basic mission statement of Zetetics requires.

Having got the basics out of the way, it will serve well to look at the three key elements of the Zetetic process in point form detail.

Premise. In establishing your premise, consider the basic elements — what you know, what you have and where you are. State what you know already and what you wish to know. State what you have now and what you would wish to have. State where you are currently and where you would wish to be.

Resolution of Doubt. Rather than simply raising a doubt over something or accepting someone else's doubt, to question should be to assess the completeness of one's own understanding of it and to ask what more can be done to fully comprehend it. This will lead naturally to the core element of question and answer.

Once you have a more conscious awareness of where you are in these sorts of terms, the initiation of a simple process of question and answer, where multiple alternative answers are considered, will help bring you to where you wish to be.

Multiple Alternative Answers. In this phase, it is vital to consider at least three alternative answers but more if they come readily. The first answer that springs to mind might seem adequate but until you have others to compare it with, you have no basis of comparison and are therefore effectively blind.

Vision is by definition having varying elements to distinguish. Having only one thing to see is like seeing only white against black as a partially blind person might so perceiving only one alternative is like intellectual blindness.

To put this all into context, it is important to consider the basic process of knowing that has been defined in broad terms in different cultures over a great deal of time.

The Basic Definition of the Process of Knowing

This was defined earliest, perhaps, by Zen Buddhism in the aphorism of the river and the mountain. "In the beginning, mountains are mountains and rivers are rivers; later on, mountains are not mountains and rivers are not rivers; and still later, mountains are mountains and rivers are rivers."

Another wording includes trees and says:

'First they seem so then they seem not so then you know them to be so.'

This mirrors the basic process of perception, doubt and resolution that Zetetics also fosters through being able to resolve thoughts well.

Given that questioning is a key element in the processes of knowing and that it is often neglected or poorly executed, it should be no great surprise to find that huge benefits can be found in applying system to it yet in fact it is surprising, and rewarding.

So because we need to be very clear about the way our consciousness works, we need to specify the three phases of knowing in detailed point form.

The Three Phases of Discovery/Knowing (3)

1 ... Presumption, or the immediate perceptions of something through seeing its most visible external characteristics.

2 ... Doubt, raised by the perception of new and sometimes seemingly incompatible factors that can lead to confusion and rejection of the thing being considered.

3 ... Resolution of seemingly disparate elements through consciously assessing any doubts that might have been raised leading to the full functional

understanding of something, in other words truly knowing what it is.

Then in alignment with the awareness of the Process of Knowing we can use zetetics to make the best possible choices, as summarized here:

1. **Questioning must be seen as more than simply doubting something and if a question is raised then the process to resolve it should be set in train.**
2. **A careful premise or verbal definition of the question, issue to be explored or desired objective must be stated.**
3. **The issue should be considered in sufficient depth to begin to provide plausible potential answers.**
4. **At least three alternative answers should be found before choosing what answer is best.**
5. **The best fitting of the alternate answers should be chosen.**

It really is very simple and so it should be. The hard part is not in the process but in the remembering to initiate it regularly, frequently in your life.

The new world that we hope for depends on all the key people involved in its establishment being able to make the best possible decisions to enable the best possible outcomes.

For that reason, please make sure you don't dismiss this as overly simple or unimportant. If you fail to consider it carefully, you could miss the point.

As a spiritual knight, you will need to be ready to effectively employ this process at a moment's notice in every important decision you make.

Chapter 13 — Identity and Social Consciousness (2)

All over the world, people have become orphaned in terms of the level of guidance they have about personal identity and social consciousness. This has catastrophic consequences for our happiness and the wellbeing of our societies, given how closely tied they are. It is one of the most important primary manifestations of the dualistic nature of this world. We are individuals and members of groups and this relationship is both complex and difficult.

Few, now, have good parental guidance on any social, psychological or philosophical matters and consequently tend to place pragmatic group priorities over the individual ones that would foster insightful self-expression and a better world.

Meaningful self-expression, a key attribute of a lucid identity, is crucial in maintaining clear identity resolution and a clear, positive identity is vital for good social relations. Given that the process of spiritual breath which is so interlinked with identity involves perception, like the physical intake of breath, and expression, like the physical exhalation of breath, a lack of adequate self-expression will lead to spiritual degradation and troubled lives without higher goals or direction.

Our material/physical existence is dualistic in nature. Every state has an opposite and the vital opposite of expression is perception. Without the smooth, cyclical interaction of both, spiritual breath falters, identity cannot manifest properly and the individual will lack conscious certainty, leading to the absence of any effective moral compass.

A strong, healthy identity is heavily dependent on conscious certainty but where certainty comes from unguided ego rather than from active enquiry and analysis (both of these related to perception and expression), it cannot possibly serve the individual reliably in the long term, nor the group. Strength in this duality of perception and expression manifests in both aspects or in neither.

Many stumble along almost blind with weak and injured identities without even knowing it. Social norms and expectations do little to correct the problem, largely because they do not take into account the dualistic relationship of the individual and society.

Some key social norms, like valuing money for its own sake and above spiritual health rather than for the constructive things it can do, greatly exacerbate the identity problem.

It is vital to change these social norms and this is where creative people are so important. Very few people have truly got what it takes to be good musicians, artists and writers/thinkers. They're rare people and it is vital that they're respected. The people who reveal the hidden meaning between life's polar opposites and craft honest reflections of life as it is and as it should be are valuable to society. As such, enduring creators should always be generously acknowledged.

The shared social world can be a maelstrom which is a challenge to understand and is difficult to stay afloat in without reference to the guidance that comes from the deeply considered self-expression of true creators. Their deeper understanding is in fact the essence of the leading edge of social consciousness.

We most directly and efficiently express and share what we perceive through carefully crafted words. The meaning that thoughtful writers reveal is crucial and has always been so throughout history.

Given that a greater command of the language can so effectively foster better understanding of how things relate to each other between the polar opposites that are so ubiquitous in life, those who cultivate it are heroes in a way that sports identities and actors never can be. Writers explore vast potentials of which conventional celebrities rarely ever begin to conceive.

In the absence of their insight, like frogs in the proverbial pot of boiling water, people fail to see how degraded things have become, especially where material wealth and its associated bravado call the shots.

Yet today, creative individuals make hefty personal and material sacrifices when they choose to step outside the arena of normal daily activity to write or to create in other ways. Risking poverty and social oblivion in this hideously corrupt landscape of 21st century Earth, they choose to do it largely because they enjoy the creative process but also because they know how crucial it is to the restoration of a healthy, fulfilling society.

Admittedly, some degree of isolation is necessary in this sort of role given that it reduces the creative person's exposure to the direct influence of social forces that tend to make people conformist.

People acting together in social cohorts will always seek to influence each other and will generally tend to repress critically important observations about polar social dynamics that may be uncomfortable or challenging either socially or individually.

Separating from the social group facilitates an individual's having 'the eyes to see' that promotes the ability to establish a clear, honest and unbiased view of things. This is crucial because there really is no other effective way to remain awake and un-beholden, and to accurately perceive the emerging trends of reality.

Disturbingly, in light of the above observation, group production of storytelling, (movies, electronic games and to some extent plays), has all but replaced quality books with the consequence that perceptual clarity has been largely sacrificed to herd emotional comfort. Unless conscious efforts are made to alter this imbalance in the dualistic framework of life, modern societies will continue to become ever shallower, more incomplete and far more miserable.

One of the most significant symptoms of this tendency to shallowness is that society becomes overly formalized, compartmentalized and rigid. Individuals suffer a lot because of this but they are also amazingly adept at finding their way around these restrictions. In fact, the conformists suffer more than the true individuals do when the most basic and traditional elements of social structure and culture are degraded.

When society fails them in one way or another, individuals get most support from their families. The main drivers of social consciousness therefore, especially in a degraded society, are families. The family is also the most effective vehicle for maintaining intergenerational expertise and development because its power base can be maintained outside the magnetosphere of social conformism.

Families are crucially important safety valves because of this but they are also the true basis of the nation. Nation is a word that primarily evokes family because it comes from the root word that means birth and therefore blood ties. So, each and every family contributes a vital set of characteristics that build the nation. They are the nation.

So, individuals, especially expressive ones, shape social consciousness and because of that the families that can nurture them are the core basis of the nation. This must mean then that the state of health of individual identities within families is absolutely crucial to the health, prosperity and happiness of a nation!

These qualities of excellent care and nurturing should not be limited to a privileged few families, whether they are business oriented or culture oriented. This is a vital aspect of social consciousness with which our long-term freedom can be assured. How could any of us know who will be the next JRR Tolkien or Dame Joan Sutherland or what family they will be born into?

Yet as things stand, significant variation both in wealth and in the health of personal identities does lead to increasingly vast divisions of wellbeing in society that must inhibit creativity. This social destabilisation adversely affects the vital state of balance between various poles and brings conditions conducive to social and national catastrophe.

It is therefore essential to deal with it — yet many feel that identity is a nebulous issue. It is talked about in the vaguest of terms and when people are asked to define their own identity, few know how to answer.

Given that, it seems crucial to discuss it and define it as well as possible.

Our identity is rooted in the understanding of our dualistic nature as both physical and spiritual beings that are social and individual with emotion and intellect driving us in an existence that can be either sleeping or waking and might have a light or dark orientation.

Beyond that, much of an individual's identity is determined by their desires — what they would like to do or would wish to happen. As such, both society as a whole and individuals should consciously acknowledge these factors, whatever they are.

With respect to these desires, it is essential to understand that we do not necessarily own our thoughts but if they remain largely unconscious, unrevealed on both emotional and intellectual levels, then they own us and control us. The fact is, we do have a dark side, and it must be owned; acknowledged or it will do harm. If we do not own it, it will own us.

Applying the same principle to the projected outcome of our thoughts, we may well end up with what we do not desire unless we are consciously aware of exactly what we do. This is true on both the social and individual levels.

Truly lucid and secure identities actually seem to be quite rare. This is a bigger problem for society than our leaders tend to acknowledge, since the ratio of secure, well-integrated people to shattered, divided and ignorant ones has to be a primary determinant of the character of national communities.

According to our dualistic nature, the most basic measure of emotional health and identity resolution is the ability to make important decisions rationally and well. This capacity vastly increases the chances of avoiding toxic thoughts, bad company, flawed decisions and actions that compromise wellbeing.

The more people with such a mind state, the less at war with itself society will be, so you should be proud if you can put the mirror up to yourself and say you do take the time to resolve apparent opposites by thinking about things in a conscious, rational way.

With at least that basic level of identity integrity, outcomes will be vastly better but there is in fact much more to a truly lucid and creative identity than the consistent use of reason.

Several subtle barriers can hinder our growth towards enjoying a stable, productive and happy identity. Fragmented thinking is the most significant factor and even people who are more rationally oriented can suffer from it. This is a form of mental disfunction in which people have incomplete, fragmented sentence structure in normal ongoing thought. It is both a symptom and a cause that results in great harm.

Unresolved thinking promotes ignorance of the spiritual aspects of life and counter-productive attitudes. This negative dynamic ultimately leads to the bizarre phenomenon of the willing rejection of the possibility of an enduring afterlife, which then creates a vicious circle of decay both moral and physical.

Yes, decay and mortality are normal parts of this dualistic world but we should still fight them and keep them in their proper zones. We wonder about why there should be death but in a dualistic framework there are always poles and death is simply one of these. We need to understand that material life has to be temporary, and therefore a stage in development, before our identity can be properly integrated.

The establishment of a coherent and consistent sense of identity has to deal with the issue of mortality because while we feel we are impermanent beings with nowhere to go and therefore nothing lasting to contribute, how can we even live life in a way that challenges the worst elements of the status quo? Why would we try to improve things?

Limited by such negative thinking, would we make the effort for the benefit of ongoing society alone because it was more enduring? Perhaps not in any real way because society, also, is impermanent, not to mention the very world itself. The fractured identities of communist ideologists deny themselves and their spirit even when this world will be nothing more than ashes in so many billion years.

The fact is, this material universe is a finite universe and we have to face it. Until we begin to consider the true spirit of creation and where it seems to lead us, we are hiding from the it and hiding from ourselves. That is poor ground for a clear and certain sense of identity.

So, we get to the matter of the drift of creation — where it all seems to be leading. Many things indicate that there is more to life than meets the eye but to tune into them, we need to focus on what seems to us to be meaningful. We need to trust ourselves and follow our own noses.

When considering the totality of creation and its higher purpose, the key factors are our intellectual and emotional flexibility — our spiritual suppleness in fact. Trusting ourselves means focusing on what we like, what we enjoy and we think is important. If we do that, we become spiritually supple.

Social programming tends to get in the way of that. Family is not always good and with undisciplined role models we can end up being ruled by unconscious behavioural traits. In the absence of conscious thought, for a mind to cause someone to behave in any particular way, programming must exist.

Most often the programming is cultural but it can also be genetic. On that score, we have long known that culturally sourced programming can be changed. The question is, can this change also be achieved with genetic programming? Does creation facilitate fundamental change?

If we are to reasonably assess that probability, we need only consider the basic strengths of the human mind; those characteristics of adaptability and ingenuity that have allowed us to develop into beings capable of shaping the planet despite our relatively small and frail physical bodies.

We are subject to the instinctive drive to eat yet some repress it to become anorexic or to participate in hunger strikes. We are apparently hard-wired to survive yet some will sacrifice their lives or endanger themselves to help others in need.

Most of us are compelled by our basic biological urges to have sex as frequently as possible but the majority of people, for one reason or another, keep their instincts well in check.

I believe that it is quite possible to alter the most basic of human behaviours to suit our circumstances so even the most counter-productive emotions must be subject to control or fundamental alteration.

Also, greater facility with emotional expression will further intellectual capacity, boosting emotional freedom again in turn.

Certainly, developing a more integrated view of the polar relationship between emotions and intellect should facilitate identity healing self-expression in us and thereby minimize the manifestation of destructive conflict at a number of different levels. All this gives weight to the argument that quantum level change is possible both for individuals and for society.

In the undisciplined thinking of modern times, emotions have been seen as innately disturbing and as competing with intellect — a vague collective conception that the more there is of one, the less there will be of the other. This attitude is the basis of a disintegrated duality — and in truth, positive emotions are more likely to support intellect rather than compete with it — the greater the emotional strength, the more powerful and lucid the intellect, as well as self-expression.

This is in fact a very powerful inbuilt mechanism to facilitate change and growth. Perhaps then we should wonder why such powerful means for change exist. If not to facilitate ultimate spiritual transcendence then what?

It bodes well but even so, it is likely that this spiritual transcendence will not be easy. Changing from one quantum state to another involves long chains of very specific actions.

Just for one thing, a clear and certain sense of self is the outward manifestation of the fact that dozens and dozens of crucial little boxes have been ticked in the process of a person's development — and there is often no easy way to know that you need to tick them off if you do not already have them.

Personal resolution to change things for the better is the first goal we need to set our sights on but this is less likely to happen in the absence of adequate definitions and revelations of the problems and without society providing the structures that will facilitate them. And for some, the need is very urgent. Given the great dangers inherent in mental instability, everyone, carer or carefree, should think deeply on the matter.

No one should assume that everything's all right, whether with respect to themselves or to anyone else that they love. Prolonged anguish, doubt and poor decision-making hold grave potential for harm even at the most basic levels. Forget all the less necessary aspects of social bullshit and pay more attention to looking after your loved ones by having 'the eyes to see'.

Clearly, there are different indicators of trouble for different people and it serves well here to consider the matter of psychological crutches — alcohol, painkillers, illicit drugs and even addiction to pathetic soap operas or random, meaningless sex. You would be most unwise to assume that any of these things are innocent. They are all potential danger signs.

If it is you in that boat, confront your issues, feel the pain and ask why it is there. Invariably, such pain will arise from some form of insecurity and when you home in on the apparent source, the most useful realization will be that the key contributor to identity security is not some quality of intelligence or wealth that you were simply gifted with by birth.

As I will no doubt say again and again there is no greater factor in spiritual development than the quality of one's internal dialogue.

Chapter 14 — The Dangers and the Cure

One of the key things in building a more constructive culture for the nurturing of individuals is that decision makers need to recognize there is more to the ability to succeed and be happy than simple energy and commitment.

Many people need help with very real problems and considerable research is needed in finding the most efficient possible means of dealing with them.

These problems are too often seen as stemming from personal weakness yet in fact they have less to do with insufficient personal effort than with the presence of a toxic social culture in by far and away the majority of this world's nations. So, if you happen to be one of those who are suffering, don't kick yourself because you're down. I hate to say it but here are plenty of others who are all too ready to do it for you.

This is a world that is painfully ignorant and uncaring of individual needs — even the long-term needs of the relatively advantaged.

A new attitude is required, especially in the halls of power but we know that will not happen without broad structural change so we need to face the fact that we will have to engineer it ourselves.

Those who would do it will need to set their minds to how to do it. Whenever decisions of cultural impact have to be made, the general character of what you truly wish to create should be addressed.

Would you wish the world to be a garden, or a wasteland? Would you wish for your national identity to be preserved or to be diminished? Would you wish to end up with a battlefield or playground? At the moment, most people have a battleground.

So, if you wish instead for your world to be a garden and a joy filled playground for you and your wonderful cherished children, the clear expression of your identity becomes enormously important, in particular as it pertains to and affects society, since so many social forces now seem to be arrayed against the worthy and the beautiful.

A secure and stable sense of identity promotes clear goals and strategies which will always be a large part of the formula for success. While most successful people have a strong identity, it does not necessarily mean that their success will be lasting or that their identity will remain resilient over time.

Those who succeed in the barren wasteland of industrial machine priorities might seem at the outset to be strong but their security, based on the material, is all too often temporary. Many who succeed initially find the going tougher later on. As their identity grows subtler and more complex, material prosperity alone will not satisfy their needs.

Just as delicate and beautiful plants might only survive in a garden that is geared to their needs, those who after a while begin to perceive the need for creative and inspirational goals cannot survive in the culture of a wasteland. Unfortunately, that is a big problem in a society where morons are given a voice and the intelligent and passionate are silenced.

Many might wither and come to nothing in such a society whereas others might mature creatively for a while, like Vincent van Gogh, only to self-destruct at the height of their creativity.

It seems fruitful then to ask how this can be changed so that humanity can be steered away from what has become a destructive and futile path.

The way things are set up in nearly all our western societies now, the devolution will accelerate quickly if not turned around soon. Most people's progress towards happiness and prosperity will be blocked. Our cultural standards and behavioural mores will continue to decay. Relationships between genders will deteriorate. Old people will be neglected even more than they are already and children will be abused in various ways as a matter of course. As a case in point, various governments, including Germany and India recently decriminalized possession of child pornography. Politicians will use a range of new excuses to further strip us of our rights. Wars will be initiated and young men will die in their millions. Such things have happened before and they can happen again.

Many of the grave ecological problems we face in the modern world will add even more material injury to the numerous insults we endure.

It is no exaggeration to say that a host of less obvious yet still very significant problems are caused by consumerist excess which is in turn caused largely by the insecurities associated with poor identity resolution. 'I feel bad so I'll just go and buy something,' is so common that it wreaks havoc. Unchecked proliferation of technology to serve materialistic goals driven by injured emotions is fuelling environmental mayhem.

People's goals largely reflect current identity attributes and the glossy, transient products of rampant consumerist industry always appeal most strongly to the insecure. We desperately need greater identity integrity but cultivating it requires a much more complex strategy than most people imagine.

In this current materialistic reality, people can be bought so easily with material things. It is really not that different to swindling land from natives with glass beads.

People give up what is truly of value to them for a whole lot of stuff that soon ends up on the trash heap and they really need to learn how to stop doing that.

The fact is, there are answers in pursuing higher goals. There can be no disputing that lack of motivation and depression hinder our willingness to change for the better but the fascinating key to all this is that chronic depression is linked to poor identity resolution, which is in turn linked to poor verbalization skills, particularly on the inside, in the private realm of our own thoughts.

This state of poor inner verbalization could almost be described as a sort of mental stuttering. We know that identity coherency is important and we know that our whole being is tied up indissolubly with language, so why do we not understand just how important inner verbal coherency is?

You might concede this but then ask what the answer is. Is it difficult? No, the best initial strategy for improving the coherency of inner dialogue is to read quality literature regularly. With that under way, then learn how to meditate. You cannot order the brain until you know how to reliably stop thoughts and start them. It's just like driving a car or flying an aeroplane. The stopping and the starting, the landing and the take-off are the hard parts and once you learn how to do that, the rest will come relatively easily.

Depression is most frequently associated with the lack of a sense of direction and what can cause such a lack but a deficiency of clear, coherent thought?

Awareness of the concept of anavah; curiosity, willingness to discover the truth and have the vigilance and diligence to act on it will aid us greatly in pursuing this internal verbal coherency.

When something generates a sense of purpose in our lives we tend to think about everything that pertains to it more carefully and we can endure almost anything in pursuing it. Without a sense of purpose, even many good things can seem bad so we more often feel bad and inevitably react to that by repressing our emotions.

Without a coherent identity, built on regular self-expression, even the simple matter of making basic life choices will become difficult. Outcomes will be more negative because other peoples' priorities will sway us unduly (as the serpent did with Eve) but it will also be difficult to see the latent potential for good in outcomes that might initially seem adverse.

In the absence of careful thought about where we are going and with the resulting lack of purpose in life, it can become all too easy to resort to sensual obsession in the form of drugs, alcohol or sex.

Eventually, we even become jaded with those experiences and that is when depression strikes.

As we begin to see the possibilities opened up by clear rational thought and how it works, it becomes more obvious why so many poor decisions are made in society. For one thing, since it is so much easier to conform than to be different, especially in the constant company of others, society is very subject to intellectual inertia.

When you are not moving forwards you are moving backwards and this applies equally to the individual and society. If too many people are weak, serpent-like powers arise to exploit these damaged incoherent identities and they do this by many ingenious mechanisms.

The current ecosystem of our social consciousness is best suited to serpent-minded, exploitative people so it should be no surprise to see such destructive, hell bent forces arising. These hidden minds like to see us afraid because then we become easier to control.

Many have seen that the recent covid crisis was more about control than anything else given the drastic increase in autocratic powers and the very low numbers of deaths. There have been some terrible pandemics of respiratory illness in recent years, one of which I suffered myself about five years ago, and these had no attention from government.

The disease I had was at least as bad as this Covid 19, probably more so. I was in my mid-fifties at the time, fit, healthy and active but it nearly killed me. Medical authorities at the time did not even want to swab me to find out what it was. I had covid five years later and it was nowhere near as bad. No, this covid pandemic response is truly about fear and control — not about helping us.

Other strategies the powers use revolve around dividing people. They have done that with this crisis also — setting the vaccinated upon the unvaccinated for one thing. One of my own near neighbours was extremely unpleasant and officious about prying into my personal health decisions and I know for a fact that I was not alone in suffering that sort of abuse.

Yet these strategies of division have been going on for decades, dividing young from old, good looking from plain, male from female, wealthy from poor, Catholic from Protestant. They use anything they can, from vaccination mandates to deceptiveness in the media and hooligan pop culture to destroy our culture and the fabric of our society.

Education is corrupted and degraded with communist values, and children are coerced into receiving vaccinations in the school system sometimes even without their parents' knowledge.

House prices are forced up artificially to provide the illusion of wealth but families are broken apart because the young cannot afford to live where they grew up.

They bribe our politicians to do their bidding on a regular basis and, as a group, cut them off from their own consciences. I know it because my father and his party colleagues in the Australian Senate were offered bribes when the international banks decided they wanted to come into Australia. Labor and Liberal politicians took the brown paper bags but the Australian Democrat senators refused them.

Australia is supposed to be a country that is tough on corruption but it is only tough on it at low levels. High level corruption is rampant here; so much so that the recent Liberal Party proposal for an anti-corruption commission while they were in government was designed to virtually ignore politicians, despite the fact that this sort of corruption costs normal hard-working Australians billions in bad decisions.

Would someone with a strong sense of identity sell out his friends and neighbours and accept a bribe? No, never. These are weak men who simply think that it will not affect them — in large part because they are already heavily damaged. The time is passed for us to accept being led by weak men.

Those who have a true sense of individual responsibility are strong already but such people must exercise their responsibility and become ever stronger. Knowing that there is a problem is always a critical phase in engineering change but given that so many folks struggle with even such basic problems as excess weight or smoking or alcohol, it is clear that finding the exact behavioural modifications and instituting consistent change will never be as easy as it seems.

No single magic bullet exists that will deal with all the individual factors behind these personal problems but there is one key tool without which we cannot find the individual solutions. Rational self-analysis. Reading and meditation lay the groundwork but disciplined reasoning will give us practical social solutions.

Reason based self-analysis is not so very complicated and we can get good practice in the process simply by applying reasoning more consistently to everyday choices. By keeping things simple at first and making reasoning work at a concrete level we can attune the mind to the process. Once it is well-established, we can then shift up and further refine our background thought processes — the most accessible and malleable aspect of identity integrity.

To consciously modify and enhance your inner verbal coherency, it is essential to regularly monitor its quality and begin to deliberately frame the thoughts in your head as if in structured sentences on paper. Think as often as you can as if you were writing it in your personal diary.

Keep doing that and make a habit of it. There are also rewards — a range of fringe benefits. The more you do this, the happier you will become and the clearer, more spectacular and more memorable your night time dreaming will be.

Knowing the problem is there is one thing but ensuring you deal with it consistently in a disciplined way is another. It ought not to be a difficult thing but in reality, because thought incoherency is both a symptom and a consequence of what lies behind you, turning that around demands a sense of the vital importance of the goal, which might in the long term even require a degree of goal restructuring.

When you see the great and noble goal ahead of you and identify yourself with it, significant change becomes possible. This is where you will begin to critically assess habitual modes of behaviour, fundamental attitudes and even long held belief systems. For some, it might necessitate the ushering in of a whole new social paradigm.

All sorts of things promise assistance in the great quest of life but ultimately most disappoint. Without a worthy mission and a true sense of direction we can only continue to flounder. We need to choose the positive alternative and be clear in our hearts about the enduring need to build a secure, coherent and resilient identity — both in social and individual terms.

Chapter 15 — The Need for a Universal Language

It has been well demonstrated that comprehensive social reconstruction is needed in society but this cannot be done without the support of others from the wider family of nations. Different national characters mean that individuals from other nations have different insights and solutions to offer us. Yet most of our brother nations in the European fold have different languages and we all suffer from greater isolation than we should because of that. Cooperation between nations and individuals is that much harder because of the language barrier and it remains so for no good reason.

There are hard times ahead and I believe that the time has come for all the Caucasian nations, in the first instance, to come together to stand and fight the growing evil that is skulking through our lands and taking us out one by one, alone.

Aloneness in a way is a natural state. Even twins go alone to the grave in the end and we generally face our most difficult problems on our own yet this is not really a negative thing. Current pop culture seems intent on making people shun and fear aloneness and self-reliance, and this is a counter-productive impetus generated by forces most vile.

The fact is, we think most clearly when we are alone, we study most effectively when we are alone, we grow most effectively when we are alone, we create things when we are alone and we are alone in sleep except perhaps while we dream.

I'm sure you get the point. Many aspects of life are experienced in solitude but in social terms we do not need to be alone so why perpetuate barriers that keep us alone more than we need to be in a way that has no constructive purpose?

The problems we face are social in both national and international terms. These are spheres of action to which aloneness has no value, except in that interaction at these levels must respect the needs the individual has for independence and frequent solitude.

Evil forces would have us be alone in more areas than we need to be and in that they would make us afraid. Would the English-speaking world have fought the Germans in WW1 and 2 if we had all spoken the same language? Would we fear the Russians now?

We fear what we do not know and how can we know people if we cannot talk to them? Fighting fear is like fighting bullies, especially in international terms — something best done communally.

Closer ties between nations of essentially similar background and genetics is a no-brainer. There is simply no reason not to build on that if we can. Pride in national language is one thing but pride in the power to build a marvellous new world of peace, health, happiness and prosperity must surely be a far greater thing.

All Caucasians are cousins of close proximity in genetic terms. My own genes are north-west European English, Scottish, Irish and Norse. These groups and many others are essentially family for me and to have them separated by unnecessary language barriers is a terrible thing. Different languages may have created subtle variations in outlook that will now be beneficial to us — but only if the communication barrier is withdrawn.

We should be able to count on each other for support and insight because of this broad bond of blood but it is difficult without communication, the third of the seven vital points in the Mindcraft Social Interaction

Canon. (Regard, Curiosity, Communication, Trust, Honour, Vigilance and Courage)

I think that most people would say they care about and are interested in their fraternal cultures but this rarely amounts to any significant interaction without regular communication. The regard is there but the subsequent steps fail without easy communication.

***

The key thing in the manifestation of care is that the ones you care about should truly care for themselves. If they do not, it is difficult to care for them even if they are within your own nuclear family.

Even close friends end up falling by the wayside if they do not learn to care for themselves. It is the primary responsibility of the individual to look after themselves first and if they do that effectively, they can then be a positive influence on the lives of other people.

Part of learning to care for oneself in this modern world is learning to be proficient in the key language of the times. Many people understand the need for a world language and most who do understand that have chosen to learn English as their second language. So much of life now is conducted in this language that it would be difficult to function internationally without it.

Business is conducted mostly in English. Culture is expressed widely and in a variety of forms in English, research finds the greatest audience in English and many of the largest, most well-funded scientific projects come from English speaking sources. Clearly, English is not yet universal but those who wish to get ahead in this new world generally learn it.

Certainly, those higher minds who would be involved with the processes of cooperation between the member nations would need at least basic English.

Given the huge potential, I do believe that English speaking nations should get together and research the best possible ways of facilitating the rapid growth of English as the primary international language, including modifying it and enhancing it intelligently.

This would facilitate and accelerate its spread throughout the world but would also coordinate ways of simplifying and streamlining it to make it both easier to learn and more meaningful.

Currently there are many strange and purposeless anomalies with the language and there are a great many meaning overlaps with words.

Our dictionaries are largely constructed in terms of providing meanings by synonym. This blurs meaning terribly and it would not be such a great task to write a conceptual dictionary where the conceptual words are described in sentences that convey the detailed nuances implied by their ancient sources or in some rare cases their popular usage.

English speaking people need to face the reality that if it is to become the world language, it must be made clearer and more accurate so that it can properly serve the needs of the world into the future.

While we, the leaders of the future, stumble about in the dark anachronism of linguistic division, those who hunt us will have a far easier job of doing so. We cannot so easily tell each other what is happening and so the atrocities continue.

So, what is going on? Are we really being hunted? You may have heard that members of a number of other races refer to the white race as the Iron Race. It seems like nothing more than a quirky oddity but when you think about the qualities of iron you think strong, enduring, invulnerable — so perhaps this is a compliment?

No, our enemies have less interest in complimenting us than in finding our weaknesses. So, what is the weakness of iron?

It rusts of course and look at the majority of our race now — subject to a host of intolerable chronic conditions. Life should be a joyous adventure but for many of us it has become a hopeless tangle of illness, psychological pressure, toxic overload, time pressure, debt and bureaucratic restriction.

That, my friends, is rust.

So, in reality we are at war and by the way, a war that we are losing. We are being cut down in a war that nobody had the decency to declare because by its nature, a war of attrition — a war of rust — can only be a secret war. It is a war that seems at first glance to be against all humanity but when you look closely at its effects, it is geared most specifically towards undermining the Caucasian race.

If you dispute the existence of this war, just look at how many fronts it is being waged on. We are under threat chemically with the toxins in our homes, in the environment, in our food, in our clothes, in our water, in our mothers' breast milk and even in the shopping dockets that we handle every day.

All aspects of the modern mainstream media are lying to us — TV, radio, newspapers, movies, magazines and popular novels — yes, even in that last bastion of honest culture, the ancient art of written storytelling.

Any truly concerned and probing authors have been carefully excluded from the crooked arena of big-time publishing. As an author, I have experienced this directly and with unabrogated consistency. No legacy publishers respond to me at all and the online platforms censor me shamelessly.

All branches of the media try to misdirect our attention and constantly reassure us that everything is all right but they certainly do not promote constructive, meaningful and truly two-sided debate. One line is presented on every issue of significance — vaccination being the stand out example — and woe betide you if you disagree because you will be labelled then as a crank, ignorant, prejudiced or simply as one prominent politician did not so long ago, a deplorable. In France, now, they have even legislated fines and long prison terms for anyone found publicly criticizing the MRNA vaccines.

In the terms of the legacy media, an anti-vaxxer has become synonymous with an ignorant moron despite the evidence becoming clearer by the day that vaccines are both dangerous and largely unnecessary. Both the gene tech and the traditional vaccines are unsafe as many expert voices have been saying for decades.

Our lives are carefully driven by the banks and the huge industrial interests they control — yes certainly in pharmaceuticals but also in areas like oil, plastics, agriculture, transport and housing.

From very early in the piece we are moulded into compliant workers and consumers and we spend most of our lives under their domination, acquiring homes, cars, clothes, gadgets, toys, holidays and so much more, most of which we rarely use. These things that we thought we valued so much often end up neglected or even in the end at the dump.

Not long after we have paid off the house, which in a decent society would be paid for much more quickly, many of us drop dead from stress, the toxic environment, isolation and our lethal pseudo health industry. Housing prices are maintained artificially high, not to benefit the investor, who after all could invest in other things, but to keep as many of us as possible on the treadmill of dependant job slavery for as long as possible.

On top of being placed on this onerous treadmill, white men are constantly under various forms of attack. They are blamed for everything bad in society, portrayed as evil (particularly blond men in almost every Hollywood movie you can think of) and presented in many forms of media as just plain stupid.

Feminism in the shape of almost universally female teachers is increasingly steering young men into trade rather than professional positions and many of those not well suited to trades work end up on the trash heap of unemployment because there simply are not enough other job avenues anymore.

Female teachers clearly have either a corrupt or an irresponsible role in this gender displacement given that, surprise, surprise, there are now so few male teachers to act as facilitators to guide boys into responsible roles.

Women now get most of the key mid-level jobs and are taught by the media to only accept men as potential partners who pretty much have everything and ironically, because of such unrealistic expectations many of our women end up alone.

Sadly, because the Globalist PC feminist line is that we should not be racist, increasing numbers of white women deal with this by opting in the end for partnering young ethnic males often with little more than basic jobs.

Meanwhile, the fertility of white males is also under threat through chemical and psychological sabotage.

White male jobs are under threat and our young men have no money. Young white males are being undermined in their capacities as future leaders and male suicide rates are astronomical. Male deaths by car crash and drug overdose are also very high. Overall, this is an appalling picture. Is it any wonder under this landslide of destructive factors that western fertility, birth rates and overall numbers are in such decline?

At the same time, in most western societies, we are being told to expect to accommodate millions of refugees from less industrialized cultures whose body chemistry has not yet been adversely affected by the chemical war zone of western life. They come in their millions and they breed fast. Their ethnic groups also ensure that they get employment, accommodation and last but not least dutiful wives, because of course *they* are allowed to keep their cultural values under the selectively applied headline of cultural diversity.

Ethnic groups get into particular employment areas and dominate them, including crucially important bureaucratic departments but no such mechanism is put in place to restore the balance for young white males whose families have lived locally for generations.

I have mentioned some of these problems before but I do so again in this new context of the language barrier because this is clearly a concerted, intense campaign against Caucasian people and I do not believe that even quite large groups in single nations alone can effectively deal with it. Getting one percent together in an active group is a hard thing and in Australia that would be 250,000 people. In rough terms, multiply that by 50 nations and you have an extremely powerful group of around 12.5 million.

There are anti-communist reformist movements in all western Caucasian nations but alone they simply do not have the power or wealth needed to combat the war being waged against them. It takes a special sort of person to lead in such organizations — to recognize and acknowledge the effects of the secret war and their numbers are too few, for now, to turn things around in their own nation states.

Also, there has been a lot of confusion about the nationalist ideal. Any nationalist knows that Globalism is against his cause but too many rule out alliance and cooperation with other worthy nations because they can so easily confuse the concept with Globalism.

All our western countries have been assaulted in the night so to speak and like Troy have let the horse in through the gates. All may be hopeless in separate language driven ignorance and isolation but there is hope because there is an opportunity here to create a great good that has never before fully come to fruit, partly because the inimical forces set against us have long tried to prevent it happening.

The unity of the Caucasian race is a key element that could hold at bay these compassionless forces. That must become our goal. The Jewish people have unity through their religion, the Chinese have it because they had the good sense to throw off the yoke of foreign invasion, the Japanese, despite some capitulation in economic terms, still maintain considerable political autonomy and racial integrity.

Many nations proudly hold onto their right to preserve their share of genetic diversity but in the west, this is somehow wrong.

If our Caucasian peoples demonstrated the same commitment to self-preservation and joined together in the creation of a great new federal nation spanning the world, we would much more effectively be able to combat the secret war of rust.

This is an exciting goal that holds great hope for us but with realization beginning to spread about the great need for this goal, you can be sure the opposition of the many that have long worked against it in the background will not stop now.

One strategy used by the forces arrayed against us to prevent Caucasian unity has been to claim that there is no such thing as a white race but no other race has complete purity in any case. Not China, not Japan, not India, yet they do much to protect their current level of racial integrity. Why should we not be able to do the same?

We have survived so far but if we do not learn to stand together, there will be so few of us in one or two generations that our enemies will easily destroy us.

There is in fact an urgent need for us to move as quickly as possible towards the creation of the United Caucasian Alliance with one unifying language, in particular for government cooperation and trade purposes, and when it has been made a reality, the fight to save the world can truly begin.

Just to be clear, I am not advocating that nations who use languages other than English should abandon their native languages. They should simply learn both, especially those people who might be involved in the noble pursuit of cooperation between brother nations. Many nations promote English as a second language already but this policy should be expanded and developed.

A United Caucasian Alliance would allow us to live as we ought to in safe, happy prosperity while preserving the key racial diversity element that has created so many amazing and wonderful things in this world.

An alliance would give us the power to order the world to save it from the current path of almost certain environmental destruction. It would enable us to take back our lives and allow us to institute well-considered compassionate measures against the threat to our racial integrity in all the qualifying nation states.

Together, enjoying a single shared language with which to collaborate for peace and justice, the white peoples could stand tall and would be capable of building a marvellous, happy, healthy new world — but divided we can only fall.

What would be different about this UCA to say the European Union? To start with, the EU administration is bureaucratic rather than political and therefore less fully accountable to the population. It has to be said also that it was started under a political system that was innately flawed and polluted with destructive anti-individual communist values. The UCA would start life with healthy nationalist values and goals.

The EU was never intended as a vehicle to unify white people and in that respect was also innately flawed. The EEC as it was known from 1958 to 1993 was principally about manipulating economics to create a power base, which has then been used to undermine racial integrity in Europe rather than to bolster it.

The whole point of establishing the UCA would be to create a union of similar peoples with the intention of maintaining their cultural and genetic diversities within discrete states. This would be achieved through regular consultation and cooperation within the mechanism of the federation. It would also cut the international banks out of the picture by establishing a shared currency and cooperative funding.

The union would allow intermarriage between individuals of its member states but would not actively encourage it. It would maintain linguistic diversity but promote cooperation and understanding by promoting

English as a universal second language. Native English-speaking peoples would be encouraged to take on a second language of their choice from the union to help maintain both the spirit of cooperation and their own relative levels of intelligence.

Striving towards establishing the UCA would require huge cooperative efforts between nationalists from different qualifying nations but those efforts would have the benefit of bringing them together in the real world as colleagues and friends.

The United States was the nearest thing we had to this and it became very powerful but it has become corrupted and it does not include other Caucasian nations.

In this age of the Internet much is said but little is done and striving towards the goal of a United Caucasian Alliance through adherence to a clear spiritual code and dissolving the language barriers would overcome the inertia and sense of despondency that is so rife in in this chaotic and uncertain time.

I believe that this approach alone will free us and lead to the wonderful future we wish for so earnestly when our hearts and minds are clear.

Chapter 16 — The Need for a Code

Multiple strategies are needed to turn around the current devolution of western societies. We are seeing grave signs of alarming degradation in many aspects of western society. Lowering educational standards and practises, degeneration of pop music into mere noise, pseudo art, dishonest one-sided media, rampant political corruption, increasing dependence on pharmaceuticals in medicine, lousy flavourless food, pollution, birth deformities and accelerating species loss just to name a few.

What most of us do not know or do not realize is that all this devolution has a point. The long-term goals of the devious architects of this mess are hidden but the least efforts of deduction scream that at the very least they wish to make us slaves in a sea of isolation and ignorance. At worst the goal is to kill us. Who? Super wealthy and powerful interests. Why? There are many possible reasons.

The need for a monarch and nobility to take ultimate responsibility for far reaching decisions that have huge effects both on us and on our world is clear. So-called democratic representatives will never own the urgent need for action and make the tough decisions that are required so we have to work to set in place the sort of people that will. This is the immediate practical side of our need but we also need to cultivate a genuine respect for nature and develop a proper appreciation for the spiritual elements in our lives.

To reorient ourselves so completely we need a code that will guide and drive the promotion of techniques that will cultivate the disciplined and honest use of intellect. In essence, it is a spiritual code that we need first and foremost, and it needs to make sense.

Napoleon gave France his French Civil Code, or Code Napoleon but this was primarily a bureaucratic document that attempted to define all important relationships between people and people and people and things. It dispensed justice determinations rather than giving us a reliable means to properly determine them.

Moreover, it has to be said that this was a vain attempt to deliver justice because its definitions were the hollow words of a tyrant — a tyrant who had killed a seventeen-year-old boy, Friedrich Staps, who had claimed that he wished to kill him.

This assassination attempt was clearly nothing more than a vain protest against injustice meted out to German states in Napoleon's Europe by a clearly incompetent minor — even as defined by Napoleon's code — yet the powerful dictator still ordered him executed.

Interestingly, The Code Napoleon dictates that a son under sixteen could be confined for up to six months for misbehaviour as determined by the father. This could continue by application for further such periods and the son had to reside with his father.

That last thing in itself would not be such a bad thing but there were no substantial restraints on the power or behaviour of the father and the only exception a son could enjoy was if he volunteered for military service after the age of eighteen. That, of course, was in the interests of the tyrant.

Predictably, this is the sort of thing that happens when the foundation of disciplined, honest thought — spiritual enlightenment — is ignored.

Within this higher discipline of spiritual understanding, we will need to devote a great deal more attention to understanding how to effectively integrate justice with compassion and intellect with emotions.

These basics of mental functionality are the key to developing a clear and coherent identity, and if most of the individuals in a society have this then the social identity will also emerge healthy.

If we are to do all the required things consistent with justice and compassion sufficiently quickly and effectively we will have to maintain constant reference to a clear code of social behaviour and spiritual standards acceptable to all.

This will be the main impetus behind the change that will steer the whole of humanity towards a future with far less pain, waste, depression and loss and with much more pleasure, creativity, joy and exciting discovery.

The carefully crafted code of Mindcraft that I referred to in chapter three is the prototype of that code. It is by no means the final word but it does encompass many vital truths and strategies that traditional religions do not. Some faiths touch on the key elements but nearly always do so with a negative slant, such as Hinduism's rejection of ego and Christianity's erroneous espousing of meekness as a virtue when the original Hebrew word really meant attentive, vigilant and diligent.

The Mindcraft of these fictional Aryan people has a wide array of different elements, some of which were introduced to you in Chapter 3. In addition to those social elements, there are the following more fundamental specifications starting on the next page that define a broader spiritual reality:

Mindcraft: the Core Knowledge of the Sacred Trees in Cloudwalker Lore.

The Vanir Cloudwalker druids of the Aryan world use trees as a metaphor for life because of the symbiotic relationship they, and we, have with them. This is important because it provides a solid natural foundation that guides the processes of our thought and reflection.

Foremost of the trees are, the ash, so important in Norse culture and the spruce, which has a conical or pyramidal shape that is very apt and useful in the matter of symbolizing the full array of the most vital elements of life. The spruce is also an apt image because it is incredibly supple and strong.

The core concepts are represented by the numbers 1 through 9 from top to bottom of the tree and the proper understanding of these core concepts in time reveal the deeper principles of Mindcraft.

1 The singularity of the spiritual source
2 The duality of material existence
3 The three phases of intellectual discovery
4 The four planes of manifest existence
5 The five elements of nature
6 The six fundamental emotions
7 The seven-point canon of social interaction
8 The eight essential attributes of leadership
9 The nine great desires

The Vanir druids in my portrayal of the Norse god's world of Arya were masters of magic and high causal thought that leads to it.

Their comprehension of the world started with the power of the singularity, which they believed was the source of all creation. That was represented by Idrasil and by the number 1 at the top of the tree.

Material reality is defined most fundamentally by the concept of duality, a key factor in the Norse creation myth, given how Muspellheim and Niflheim came together over time to form the ancient god Ymir, and it is represented by the number 2.

The way people engage with this reality is by discovering and learning, and this process has three basic stages — assumption, doubt and resolution represented by the number 3.

As learning opened up, the Vanir acolytes began to see that it was necessary to define and appreciate the four different planes of existence that must be dealt with in interaction with life. These four planes are of course, the material, the physical, the astral and the causal, and are represented by 4.

The Vanir also believed in four basic elements of earth air, water and fire plus the ethereal or the intangible and this set of elemental definitions helped their students understand the way they interact with the physical and material world. This was represented by 5.

The Vanir understood the intellectual in terms of the basic process of discovery seen in 3 but they also see it as necessary to define and include emotions to balance this. The core emotions number 6.

The already mentioned basic canon of social interaction so vital to leading life well in this world includes seven key elements represented by 7.

A further set of definitions of required leadership attributes number 8.

Lastly, the core group of fundamental desires that drive people on their journey through life and which reveal so much about human nature number 9.

And so, you have the basic pyramidal structure of the Jastara spruce.

The nine levels of the tree require some further explanation, which follows below.

The Singularity

The Vanir druids saw the great tree of Idrasil as the pure singularity from which all manifest energy and substance comes. It is regarded both as a mystical source of divine inspirational energy and the fundamental source of all creative energy that made the manifestation of the material world possible, along with the very maintenance of its existence in every moment of time from the beginning to the end. It is also regarded as both a source of physical and emotional energy.

The Duality

The duality is seen in every aspect of material manifestation from night and day to genders. The understanding of the relationship between dual opposites is seen to lead to comprehension of the finer points of philosophical understanding of existence and the revelation of many hidden truths.

The Three Stages of the Intellect

The druids, along with many other cultures, understood the basic process of the intellect as having three main stages. Assumption, doubt and resolution. Most people see something and assume that it is just as it appears. On closer or longer examination, incompatible, surprising or conflicting elements of its makeup are revealed and doubt about the true nature of the thing is generated.

Upon careful consideration of all the elements of something's makeup and its duality relationships, a proper understanding of the thing is established and doubts are resolved.

The Four Levels of Existence

The druids understand that the material, the physical, the astarin or astral and the causal are the four fundamental levels of existence which need to be taken into account in order to truly understand true desires, destiny and justice. Every level has its rules and its secrets and they believe that no one can fully understand their existence without taking into account all four levels.

The Five Elements of Nature

The druids perceive that the five elements of nature are land, air, water, fire and the ethereal or intangible. They believe that the proper understanding of the elements allows interaction with the elements' spirits and fosters a greater understanding of our existence and our nature within the framework of these fundamental elements, as explained by Thor and Freja in their conversations about the nature of the elements.

The Six Core Emotions

The six fundamental emotions come in dualistic pairs. The first pair is love and hate or disgust. The second pair is peace or contentment and anger. The third is curiosity and ignorance. All of these amount to either acceptance or rejection. They are three basic dichotomies of acceptance and rejection that relate to the personal world of our inner being, the social world and the material world — the three main spheres people engage with during their lives.

They need to be defined in such basic terms because recognizing the source of the feelings and individual experiences helps him come to terms with them.

The Seven Prime Elements of Social Interaction

The druids understand that the crucial seven-point canon governs human relationships. The seven elements are:

Regard
Curiosity
Communication
Trust
Honour
Diligence
Courage

Each of these is the foundation for the next and the dedicated execution of each builds prosperity and happiness for all.

Regard is usually the starting point for meaningful long-term relationships and if accompanied by curiosity often leads to communication.

After a period of increasing communication, trust is built and eventually circumstances are encountered which might challenge that trust.

In dealing with those circumstances properly, honour is built and with the diligent maintenance of that honour comes the courage to do things right even in the face of challenge and adversity, knowing that the honour built between friends and allies will help to sustain and support you in these actions.

The Eight Requirements for Noble Leadership

1. The responsibility to demonstrate compassion for his fellow man.
2. Loyalty to family and nation manifesting right through to ensuring quality succession.
3. The honesty to respect perception and the discovery of truth through intellectual rigor.
4. The diligence to learn and find the right way.
5. The vigilance to perceive and foresee potential dangers.
6. Adherence to a comprehensive coherent spiritual code.
7. Present well in a reassuring and unthreatening manner.
8. Love and trust life enough to be courageous in the face of adversity.

The Nine Great Desires and the Significance of Desire

The druids taught that the old corrupted concept of sacrifice was only designed to delude people and trick them into accepting wrong notions and a poor deal in life. They assert that room must often be made in peoples' lives for new things by relinquishing other things but they do not deny the power, the meaning and the spiritual growth potential of true desires.

Desire is seen as one of the main driving forces in the journey through life and, along with ego, if it is repressed too much, consciousness will be stifled. Consciousness needs desire, given that it is the main emotion associated with achieving goals and given that achieving goals is integral with the process of maturing conscious intellect.

In other words, desires provide grist for the mill, mentally. Desires reflect our eternal inner being and as such they are completely just and healthy to pursue in a reasonable and self-aware fashion. They both enliven and educate the spirit and any attempt to persuade people to divorce themselves from desires is simply a con.

The druids say that we learn more about our desires by understanding that they are all offshoots of the nine great desires that stem from the three fundamental ones. Initially, from the desire for love comes romantic desire, the desire to please and serve friends and family and ultimately the desire to know boundless love. From the desire for wealth comes the desire for prosperity, the desire for security and the desire to influence people. From the desire for power comes the desire to take what you want, the desire to hold what you have and the desire to institute positive change.

The first branch from each is much the same as the core concept. Each of the further two extensions from the fundamental desire represents a development from the first, a step up in sophistication and personal growth, but all desires are important and no worthy desire should be ignored. They work together and are a part of the same whole. Yet it must be borne in mind that obsessions are not desires and can conflict with the fulfilment of true desires.

If you're unsure about the functional difference between obsessions and desires, reference is made to it in 'Kill the Bull: in the Resolution Individual Identity', which deals with these sorts of concepts in greater depth.

In a way, desire is the 0 as well as the 9 because it is what drives people to fulfil their destiny by learning all of what lies between their drive and their destiny. Desire is what completes the circle and allows the individual to ultimately transcend his limitations.

The Philosophical Essence of the Druids' Lore

Premise:

There is an individual and a society of individuals and every society should aim to facilitate the individuals' journeys through intellectual and emotional understanding towards the higher state of spiritual awareness.

The group is there to serve the individual in a balanced way to provide physical and material security that furthers the positive relationship between the temporal and the spiritual.

On this journey, both the individual and the society must acknowledge that careful thought and control of the mind are the only reliable sources of personal power and fulfilment.

Consciousness is increased when careful thought is used to reveal structure and meaning, which the Norse God, Odin, constantly sought, and when control of the mind fosters respect for truth.

Higher knowledge encompasses both the manifestation of structure and meaning and the awareness of it, and therefore the mind, through careful thought, can rule over matter.

Basic Levels of Existence:

1. The singularity
2. The causal
3. The astral
4. The physical
5. The material

Elements of Existence:

1. Intangible or ethereal
2. Air
3. Water
4. Fire
5. Land

Basic Functions of Existence:

1. Curiosity
2. Ideas
3. Feelings
4. Movement
5. Social interaction

Basic aspects of existence:

1. The soul of the individual.
2. The intellect of the individual.
3. The emotions of the individual.
4. The body's parameters.
5. The body's interactions with the world.

Relationships of Levels, Elements, Functions, Aspects

1. singularity/intangible/curiosity/soul
2. causal/air/ideas/intellect
3. astral/water/feelings/spirit
4. physical/fire/movement/physical body
5. material/land or earth /social interaction/the world

Basic Laws of Interaction:

1. The emotions serve the soul.
2. The intellect serves the emotions.
3. The body serves the mind, a smooth synthesis of emotion and intellect.
4. The material world serves the body.
5. The body nourishes the material world.

Basic definitions:

1. The soul outlives the body and is nourished by spiritual, emotional and intellectual experiences.
2. Emotions can be both obvious and subtle and give meaning to life through contributing structure and memory to soul.

Emotions choose overall direction and intellect determines the best way to get there.

3. Intellect is strengthened when it is used to support emotions, lifting the mind to focus on the more enduring, meaningful level of causal perception relating to purpose, structure and meaning.
4. The body enhances the intellect through giving structure to experience and should be maintained rigorously to maximise inspiring experiences.
5. The material world is symbiotic with our physical forms and must be cared for as an extension of our bodies.

Things to Consider about the Above Basic Definitions:

The Soul

1. The soul retains memories between lives so make sure to make the memories as good as possible.
2. The soul is eternal; therefore, it is vital not to fall into the trap of boredom but instead to cultivate curiosity and appreciation in all things.
3. Nurturing the individual soul will eventually release it from the material into causal awareness and furthering this process should take precedence over all other things.

The Emotions

1. The emotions are building blocks of spirit and spirit is what builds and gives structure to the soul, allowing it to eventually manifest on the more complex and permanent causal plane.
2. Emotions can be enhanced by focusing intellect on things that reveal and support them.
3. Desire is the main driving emotion that gives us direction and it should be cultivated rather than suppressed.
4. Higher spiritual knowledge employs purposeful strategy to encompass the bigger picture of structure and meaning.
5. Clear emotions support perception.
6. Clear emotions support expression.
7. Perception and expression are the inward and outward breaths of conscious, causal existence.

8. Clear emotions support intuition and other subtle mind powers.

The Intellect

1. The intellect is a tool of awareness, not consciousness itself.
2. Consciousness can apply focus to intellect to make it stronger.
3. The intellect builds, supports and applies structures known as concepts.
4. The intellect can use a process of inner dialogue to help establish a coherent world view.
5. The more conceptual structures available, the more powerful the intellect.
6. The intellect should be used to support the perception and expression of emotion and to facilitate its goals.
7. The intellect should choose with care when, where and how emotions are expressed.
8. The intellect can be used to facilitate making choices.
9. The intellect can be used to discover truth.
10. The intellect can be used to choose positive standpoints.
11. Higher and higher levels of truth must be explored to make better choices in the search for structure and meaning.
12. Aspiring to the greater goal of causal awareness through seeking knowledge with rational choices is intellectual breathing and it creates a spiritual flame, which is, in a more complete sense, being on fire with life.
13. Concentration should be understood as centredness rather than effort.

The Physical Body

1. The body is temporary.
2. The body requires careful maintenance.
3. The body is a filter for experience in the material world.
4. The body powers the intellect.
5. The body will only properly support the intellect if the intellect is used to maintain it effectively.
6. The body is powered by breath, water and food in order of importance.

7. Breath connects us most immediately with life and the manner of it reflects the quality of our connection with life.

The Material World

1. This world is a world of duality in which everything has an opposite and awareness of the balance between them must be maintained.
2. The material world is temporary.
3. The material world is in a constant state of flux and can fool the physical senses because of that.
4. The world supports us and we must support it.
5. The world nurtures the ultimate maturation of our souls when we choose to focus on higher spiritual knowledge over material manipulation — the creation of objects.
6. Material manifestation of objects can occur without taking into account the bigger pictures of balance and causality.
7. The world reflects us and can be poisoned just as we can.
8. The world has a consciousness.

Application of Mindcraft / Dragon Lore in the World

Key Areas

1. Worship
2. The Law
3. Leadership
4. Relationships
5. Education
6. Culture and Creativity
7. Agriculture
8. Health

Key Things to Remember in These Areas of Application

Worship

1. Worship is a private matter between the individual and the divine.
2. Worship should be reflected in daily life by how you treat all things.
3. Worship should be done with the will for self-improvement and causal understanding.
4. Worship should be done with the awareness of all four primary levels of existence.
5. Worship should not have attention drawn to it in any way.
6. Keep faith with the evident purpose of the divine.
7. Idrasil helps those who help themselves and those around them.

The Law

1. All human laws should be enacted with respect primarily for the spirit of the law.
2. The law should support the happy, safe, fulfilling and healthy lives of individuals.
3. The law should not be overly complex.
4. The law should express both compassion and care.
5. The law should be understood by all.

Leadership

1. Leadership must be responsible, mentally disciplined and honest.
2. Leadership has to be enduring to be responsible.
3. Leadership succession should be carefully planned.
4. Successors should be chosen from a substantial group of heirs.
5. Leadership must employ an integrated chain of two-way communication with subordinate levels.
6. Leadership must embody both curiosity and compassion.
7. Leadership should delegate responsibility but maintain oversight.
8. Strong leadership should liberate individuals.
9. Leadership should make the most of individuality.
10. Leadership should not forbear responses to damaging irrational actions.
11. A leader must calculate potentials rationally yet know that the choice must sit right with his heart.
12. A leader must understand that justice means 'the right way'.
13. A leader should lean towards tempering resolve with mitigating kindness.
14. A leader must ensure that his nobles are worthy.
15. A leader must work for unity.
16. A leader must seek to understand the perspective of others.
17. A leader must understand that proper regard promotes curiosity, communication, trust, honour, vigilance and courage, and as such is the foundation of peace and prosperity.
18. A leader must love his people and facilitate their ultimate causal awareness.

Relationships

1. People are all different and their needs should be understood and met through good communication.
2. Relationships are all difficult, primarily because of the conflicting interests of the need for social interaction and the need for solitude.
3. Every relationship has a leader.
4. Every relationship must be conducted carefully.
5. No relationship obviates responsibility for actions.
6. A good relationship will reflect awareness of the seven-point canon of social interaction: Regard, Curiosity, Communication, Trust, Honour, Vigilance and Courage, each one leading to the next.
7. Love must be supported by ongoing care both for overall health and higher development.
8. Plural marriages can promote good relationships when conducted in the right spirit.
9. If you wrong someone you must make amends.
10. People should be valued over things.

Education

1. People should be taught to learn how to learn.
2. Education should be inspirational rather than manipulative.
3. Education should aim towards causal awareness.

Culture and Creativity

1. Society should value creativity in people highly.
2. The value of creativity should be ranked in terms of how it serves conscious awareness, the forms supporting awareness of the highest three levels of existence (the singularity, causal, astral triangle) being valued the highest.
3. Cycles of perception and expression should be represented in creative things.
4. Creativity should express and enhance causal understanding.
5. Creativity demonstrates and facilitates proximity to the divine — the ultimate creator.

Agriculture

1. All agricultural activities should be clean and sustainable.
2. Agriculture should be as safe as possible for all.
3. All methods and practises should care for the world.

Health

1. All health systems should be primarily preventative.
2. All health practises should focus on causes over symptoms.
3. All health practises should take into account the priority of conscious awareness.

Primary Rules of Mindcraft to Support a Healthy Relationship with Life

(The primary rule set, which roughly equates to the Ten Commandments, while not supplanting them, except that there are twenty-one)

1. Test assumptions with careful thought.
2. Acknowledge that personal growth never ends.
3. Read widely and regularly.
4. Perform the spirit cast daily. (meditation to still the mind)
5. Cultivate methodical reasoning.
6. Make your choices conscious by selecting from a considered range of alternatives.
7. Establish a daily agenda of issues to consider and discuss.
8. Exercise the imagination.
9. Sing.
10. Envision a higher, causal existence.
11. Live in harmony with the world and other individuals.
12. Seek the good in things.
13. Battle evil and wrongdoing wherever necessary.
14. Consciously regulate breathing at least three times a day.
15. Fulfil true desires.
16. Resolve doubts rather than dismissing them.
17. Cultivate arcane skills to enhance causal awareness.
18. Be open to communication.
19. Cultivate love and good humour.
20. Seek a sense of fun, adventure and delight in all you do.
21. Seek excellence in all that you do.

First Lesson for the Acolyte, having read the above.

The Mindcraft adept will recognize that we can change destiny, not because we would have it one way or another but because we make the best possible choices and work hard to discover the structural meaning and purpose in the situations we face.

These are the basics of Mindcraft Lore but the full understanding of the concept is built gradually and conveyed more completely in The Reign of the Dragon series of novels.

The druid code stands against the materialistic code of the usurping Meccanat administration and the finer points of its understanding are revealed gradually in the novels as they are to the principal characters in their complex and challenging lives.

Those novels are the fruit of more than twenty years' work and their complete understanding cannot be adequately summarized in a few paragraphs.

Yet having such a code is an indispensable part of restoring social culture and building a better future. In the twelfth and currently last of the Reign of the Dragon books, Odin's Genesis, Thor tells wayward leaders on the magical planet of Genesis that they need a comprehensive code to bind them, as follows:

'You need a code ... a bond … or latent envy will darken (your) spirits. A strong code will tie you together and make you all part of something bigger than yourselves.'

Then a little later:
'It is essentially the art of interaction between the individual and his surrounding environment and between the individual and other individuals. This is, as many Ellarans understand it, the art of Mindcraft.'

There is of course much more to this code of conduct and many more observations are made in the series concerning such topics as consciousness, spirit, leadership and destiny.

With such a code, we can have a valuable chart to assist us in steering the vessels of our lives on the great ocean of material existence.

Chapter 17 — Leadership in the Family

In earlier chapters, I introduced the concept that family was the basis of the wider family we know as the nation and how a good leader has to accept the existence of a wider family to which he owes allegiance.

Yes, good, effective, honourable and loving leadership is essential at the national level but it cannot happen without first being present at the family level. The family comes first and if the family is no good the nation cannot be any good.

A strong family has two loving parents but also ideally grandparents, uncles, aunts, cousins and friends. The more isolated families there are, the less structure and strength there is in the nation. Traditional roles hold great value in the family and in the nation.

Assertiveness and accommodation are fundamental characteristics strongly aligned with gender in family relations and acknowledging their role is enormously important. There may be times when they rotate between genders but in good family relationships this will be the exception rather than the rule. They begin within the family then later extend into courtship.

If these natural roles are undermined in each gender by spurious and falsely progressive ideas about equality, which in modern leftist, globalist terms has come to mean sameness, then courtship becomes much harder and less likely to have positive results.

Men should be assertive, which involves proposing actions of desire, interest or worth, while women should contribute to coherent, constructive outcomes by being receptive and responsive, as well as willing to negotiate.

This intelligent receptiveness can be achieved through a strategy of being engaging, complimentary and expressive. In other words, matters raised by men should not be blocked or dismissed out of hand nor, God forbid, accepted without question.

A woman's verbal responses to suggestions should be analytical rather than confrontational or even directly agreeable. Even points of agreement should be explored in the spirit of zetetics to help bring further and more suitable alternatives to the table. In other words, couples should converse rather than order and obey.

If a woman wishes to build and maintain a rapport, conversation will assist her. If the conversation does not progress very far during courtship, no harm will have been done and both parties will become aware that there may be a basic incompatibility as partners. Yet a link of friendship might well have been forged and friends are always valuable. If, however, the conversation continues and develops, you might have the beginnings of a rapport that will build a family.

Creative unity starts with the family and the ideal family is no foregone conclusion. No matter how well brought up, people will always have problems adapting to the role of partner and then of parent. Neither are simple things but more and more, government seems to want to interfere and make it even harder.

As parents or principal carers, people experience many challenging situations that would be unlikely in the role of secondary 'weekend' parents or extended family relatives. There is also a sense of immense and ongoing responsibility that can become wearying, especially if both parents are fighting for the upper hand while jousting for supremacy with indistinguishable roles in a world gone crazy with obsession for sameness.

Many new parents can become overwhelmed by the diverse problems and burdens of responsibility. This is especially onerous in our modern world where gender roles have become so confused, where extended families or clans barely exist and where the demands of work make such great inroads into personal lives.

It is even worse for single parents. The ideal is two committed parents and a close extended family. Clearly, rearing children is really a job for two so single parents will find the problem list large and the solution list correspondingly small.

Thankfully, there are some practical and acceptable solutions. If there is one thing that any writer should be able to say with conviction, it is that communication is the key to solving problems, and communication happens best when two people approach a problem from different angles and perspectives — parent to parent or parent to child.

If two parents approach things from the same perspective they argue over trivialities rather than having constructive debates over real issues.

Yet even in the face of the deepest conflicts there are usually intelligent solutions to be had. Sometimes the stimulus of challenge and conflict can push the mind into a higher gear, especially if the conflict is over resolving a real issue rather than a triviality.

Within this scenario, you can transform obstacles into useful handholds, especially when you come at it with the vigour and determination that pride in a particular role will afford you.

Amusingly, the ancient Tantric tradition gave considerable guidance in the art of lovemaking, which in many cases leads to having children and all the ensuing problems — but it also saw fit to offer guidance in solving the subsequent problems using the same idea of transforming obstacles.

Parenthood can make people or break them and if a host of tragedies are to be avoided, parents must come to terms with the unavoidable facts of the situation. The learning curve new parents face is steep and many of them, particularly men, opt out after a while. Such avoidance of responsibility might be understandable but it does not make it right, even if the father does not disappear completely from his child's life.

The disgust that many women feel for men who abandon them, psychologically or materially, to deal with everything on their own, is understandable.

It might be complete or it might be partial but either way it is wrong. Fortunately, it is not universal. Many men have left then seen the error of their ways.

Life would become very hard if the majority failed to change for the better at least a little. People learn, as parents, deeper and faster than at any other time in their adult life. The key point is that people should be able to enjoy that learning, just as they would if they were learning to dance, abseil or ski.

To properly enjoy any situation, people have to have some certainty over the role they play, the rights that gives them and what they can be proud about. With that constructively gender aware frame of mind, it should be possible for both men and women to enjoy spending time with children.

Most people will probably remember at least one subject at school that they did not enjoy. Nine times out of ten that subject would have been one that they did not understand and had difficulty coming to grips with. Well, in this difficult subject of parenting, there is considerable expertise available, although a more confusing array could hardly be possible to imagine. Many experts have conflicting approaches and some obviously manifest a deficiency of real experience concerning what happens when the chips are really down.

A new parent soon realizes that there is a lot more to the job than meets the eye. Love accompanied by comprehensive care for a child is never automatic but for several reasons, buckling down to it is a more complex and involved process of adjustment for a male than it is for most females. This is why the matter has to be discussed in the wider context of building a new and better society.

Men have been increasingly ignored and sidelined in our modern societies but their willing input is essential if we are to bring about positive social change. If we are to be successful in engineering positive change, men will have to drastically alter their expectations of lifestyle and activities. They are, in general, brought up without much focus in the area of childrearing and relating to small children.

It can be difficult for men to tune into small children and very difficult for them to switch off from the sorts of pursuits and activities that might get in the way of that tuning in process yet men must accept the challenge of family if we are to build a better world. This is a great example of sacrifice being necessary only to make way for new things.

How a father and mother respond to having children is a key element of what makes a nation so we need to get it right. The basics should be defined and rigorously checked off against one's own experience. Parenting is also steeped in emotion and it can be all too easy to fool ourselves about our adequacy.

In the end, the only way to consistently tune into a very young child is to take their lead. This is harder before the child learns to talk but the more it is done, the more quickly the child will learn to talk. It is essential to take the time to listen and focus on the child. This can be very rewarding when you choose to do it but difficult when *they* demand attention. Every parent has to learn to sacrifice their time and in many ways, their independence if they are to make the most of family and contribute a proud part of the nation.

Even when the child learns to speak, the process is quite involved. It is vital to answer children's questions with as much pertinent detail as possible or they will not be satisfied. They are not merely filling in blanks. They are communicating with love and they expect their parents to return the compliment.

When parents have to place limitations on young children, the reasons for it should be fully explained to them. It is amazing how beautifully such efforts can be rewarded with delightful childlike observations of innocence, clarity and even genius.

By way of example, many years ago, as a young man, I was selling my Landcruiser and had to take it out for a demo run while looking after both my children. On the way, my six-year-old son sat between the young woman inspecting the car and myself. My seven-year-old daughter had to sit in the back on her own.

On the return trip, Nicole, a kind and attractive young woman in her mid-twenties, was conscious of the need to do the right thing and sat in the back next to my daughter. My son saw it as a rejection. He decided to play pissed off. "I don't like you anymore" he blurted out. "You never liked me anyway."

I had three options, as I saw it. One was to tell my son to be quiet and behave, the second was to deliver a good hard smack, and the last was to enter into a lengthy explanation of the implications and consequences of the situation. I knew straight away that the first option would not work and that the second would likely be counter-productive in the long term. It was awkward and time consuming to employ the third option but in the end, I bit the bullet and got on with it.

I explained to him that it was only fair our new friend should sit next to his sister because she had not enjoyed the benefit of her company before.

Seeing a degree of inflexibility still in his face, I proceeded to tell him that it was important for him to learn what was fair so that people would like him and would always be happy to be his friend. It might have seemed obvious but children do need to be reminded quite a lot in the face of new or challenging circumstances, about the way things work.

Having bitten the bullet, I found that the process of explanation in that situation did not turn out to be all that lengthy or difficult and that the observations had almost suggested themselves.

It occurred to me later that having some standard lines drawn from some sort of story-telling to introduce this sort of conversation would make it even easier — like "Now, I've got something to say on this matter my young Padawan, and you know that it will help you if you listen carefully," or some such thing.

That way, it would always be quicker and easier to get constructive thoughts off the ground, also gaining precious seconds to think about the essence of the particular problem.

Getting back to the story, my son thought about the situation for only a few moments before turning around and speaking again to Nicole. He said then, very clearly and succinctly, 'I'm sorry I looked at you through my bad eye. I have a good eye and a bad eye and now I'm going to see you through my good eye.'

Nicole was astonished and delighted. So was I. The remarkable thing was that a boy of six could have the ability to render objective his emotions, to stand back from himself and see where he was coming from. There was also the simple yet beautiful way in which he defined his own behaviour.

That incident was one of the positive ones. They were not all so notable but when someone does their best to love another who is in a state of conflict instead of slapping them down, they uplift them and help them to become capable of great things, no matter who they are, children or adult, male or female.

Certainly, the same principles should be applied to running nations. If our leaders treat their people like naughty, uncontrollable children by slapping them down, many will take on the role of rebel and run with it. Then the nation has more problems rather than less.

Kindness and friendship are the keys — and parents can be friends to their children. Friendship comes with regard, affection and trust and does not need to be bought with things. Friends can also be leaders and why would they not lead their friends also?

Given that friendship is won first with regard then cemented with the six other elements of the seven-point canon, is it not the whole point of facilitating social interaction? Yes, friendship is one of the principal goals of a good life but unfortunately, many spoil the social groundwork by faking their regard, for indeed not all people can be friends.

There will always be conflict but as elucidated in 'The Art of War', we have a great deal to learn from our enemies as well as our friends and if we cannot allow ourselves to face the reality of having enemies, we lose a vital dimension of life.

Moreover, it is vitally important how we treat our enemies. We should treat them in many respects just like our friends. We should be honest, up front and vocal about our points of contention with them and entirely scrupulous.

There are so many complex challenges and demands in life that it can be difficult to hold the awareness of the need to give in such a basic way, to enemy or to friend.

The love you hold in your heart for family and friends, your shared experiences, the growth that comes from the challenges you set yourself, your abilities and your own self-understanding are the truly significant things in the long run.

Leadership in families can be very difficult but being a father or mother of a family can also be amazingly rewarding. Mostly, we simply need to be aware of the beauty and pleasure of play.

Bathing in the source of inner energy through meditation also fosters laughter and playfulness, a vital happy flow of energy and expression that is universally admired. It allows you to play and to play is the first principle of love. It is the epitome of interaction and good relationships in life are built that way.

It is vital to point out, however, that there is more to play and to love than innocent frolicking. Neither can they be universal or indiscriminate.

Playfulness actually involves both like and dislike. Being clear about what is liked and what is not liked is crucial to creating love in any sphere of interaction, bearing in mind that there is a very real distinction between dislike and indifference.

Dislike is a natural, positive and healthy reaction to things or people that is only dependent on sound judgment for its validation but plain indifference is of no value to you or anyone else.

Active dislike can be a catalyst for positive change where change is necessary and can lead to wonderful experiences. After all, you have to establish definite views about things before you can change or develop in any positive way.

Dislike is active, alive and honest, whereas indifference comes from being forced to always like things and therefore denies the potential for change. In this way, dislike is a very real part of love.

Awareness of the negative dualities in your emotional spectrum can lead to valuable insights into acceptable standards of behaviour in any sphere, including friendship.

If you want to lead a family well, you'll need to do it with love. By the same token, if you want to lead a nation, the same applies.

Everyone would like to be loved, admired and respected but few know how to consciously generate such positive reactions on a consistent basis but in simple terms, you get what you give.

The more awareness we have of the dynamics of the connection between everyone, the better we will understand that love is not an airy-fairy goodwill-to-all kind of feeling. This is where lots of well-meaning dads get it wrong and get left behind.

Love is a battle. It is fire and water. It is a play of conquest and surrender, advancing and yielding. Where there is any real love, there will have been doubts, challenges and eventual understanding.

If there is no exchange of potent emotions, there cannot be any love but before the interplay can begin something has to be laid on the line. Usually, something has to be risked for something else to be gained.

With love, people lay their hearts on the line by being open in their communication with another, perhaps by expressing more of their hopes, desires, ambitions and fears than they otherwise would.

You alone can turn the switches of attitude within and open the gateways of trust that social challenges demand. It might seem difficult but a regular soaking in the energy of the inner singularity using meditation will make such generosity much easier.

People generally think they have got only so much power to love life, to love themselves or to love anyone else but consistent meditation reveals a vast replenishing pool of positive energy within.

Resources in the external world are finite, mental effort not the least. Leading a family can drain that resource hugely so it is vital to learn how to access that pool of energy deep within and thereby to cultivate an environment of enthusiasm in your life.

Once you have the energy and have the belief that there is purpose to life, it is easier to see that over time, everyone can have a very positive effect on each other. This is one of the best and most efficient ways to expend mental effort.

There is great potential for the creation of positive energy in one individual but little capacity for the storage of it, whereas the social organism is like a vast power cell. Everyone contributes to it and the energy level of it is felt, deep inside, by all.

Chapter 18 — The Failure of Religions

It has been said by a number of modern conservative commentators that Christianity will save society from degradation but others have a more subtle and intelligent view requiring us to deeply reassess what is of value and what is not.

As it stands, and as it is practised by many modern Christians, Christianity will not save us. In fact, it is a big part of the problem and I will tell you in this chapter exactly why. It is vital to cover this aspect of society in a reasonable degree of detail because many are still, to their loss, under the sway of deeply irrational interpretations of scripture.

Christianity is the main religion in my society so I will deal with it first and primarily. In the first instance, it was perverted by early Roman influences. Constantine presided over the Council of Nicaea to create a vehicle for social control in the Roman Catholic Church and virtually every offshoot of that flawed seed carries crucial errors to this day.

What are those errors?

1 Promulgation of fear.
2 Peddling conformism.
3 Interpretation of myth/allegory as literal fact.
4 Deifying Jesus against his own word.
5 Interpreting the bible with modern cultural bias.
6 Praying in public against Jesus' direct instruction.
7 Idol worshipping, mostly in the Catholic tradition.
8 Discouraging truly spiritual values in daily life.
9 Alignment of church leadership with autocratic political leadership.
10 Inciting relinquishment of individual responsibility.

11 Mistranslation of ancient texts.

12 Obsessive pursuit of money, power and things.

These are the top twelve elements of failure in Christianity. One for each of Jesus' disciples as it happens. There are others but these are the main ones and they are certainly enough to undermine a religion to the point that it has no value — in fact so that it has a strong negative value.

Some branches of Christianity do not manifest all of these negative fruits (by their fruits you shall know them) and evil things (a good man out of the good treasure of the heart bringeth forth good things: and an evil man out of the evil treasure bringeth forth evil things.) but I know of none that do not manifest any of them. Each one is a fatal error that will inevitably lead to misunderstanding, social division and some atrociously poor decisions.

While I do not condemn those who follow such flawed beliefs, I do condemn the religions that purvey them and at times, the behaviour of those who follow them. I believe in calling a spade a spade and care nothing for the warped elements of the traditions that have so long misguided us — to the point where we are now seem close to engineering our own imminent destruction.

First of all, religion is or should be a private thing for very good and clear reasons, as Jesus himself said when he told us to pray in our bedrooms with the door shut. Given this, if it is organized religion, it's bad. If Jesus was alive today, he would be horrified.

Just by that one measure alone, just about every organized religion fails to acknowledge the truth and fails to comprehend the essentially private nature of communion with the divine. Nothing can go right from that flawed pattern and these powerful religions can only be seen as the proverbial houses built on sand or as the poor fruits.

Once people give up the wrong, conformist behaviour typically associated with these organized religions, they can use their own brains and begin to perceive things as they are instead of how they have been taught to see them. With that, many of the instructions of the stiff self-righteous dogma mongers that have dominated them will be seen as misleading and will be done away with.

Some of these conformist views come from Constantine's warped church but others come from ancient texts that have been misinterpreted.

In particular, while the Hebrew books of the Old Testament do include some interesting elements from which one can pry valuable insights, even in the matter of intellectual resolution, some aspects of their ancient culture were bizarre or even cruel. This might lead to presumptions by modern Christians that these bizarre ancient ways were authorized by God.

Incest, for example, is portrayed as practised by some great biblical figures yet is it really acceptable? Yes, it's an extreme example but sometimes extreme examples are most apt for making points clearly.

Perhaps the positive elements are there in some of the Hebrew writings because they derived much of their thought and culture from ancient Greek philosophy, and if so, this is fortunate, as long as we properly understand and acknowledge these vital elements.

According to Edward Gibbon at the end of Chapter 21, part 1 in Decline and Fall of the Roman Empire, much of this ancient Hebrew wisdom was borrowed from Plato's understanding of existence.

Gibbon says: "One hundred years before the birth of Christ, a philosophical treatise, which manifestly betrays the style and sentiments of the school of Plato, was produced by the Alexandrian Jews, and unanimously received as a genuine and valuable relic of the inspired Wisdom of Solomon."

Much of the wisdom in the bible, the Catholic Church stole from the Jews who in turn borrowed it from Plato, the greatest philosopher of all time — but when it comes down to us, those who would control us for their own ends have twisted it around to mean exactly the opposite of what it should.

One riddle in the Bible has attracted much attention over the years and I will use this to demonstrate the hidden power of some of these ancient scriptures that have been so perverted towards conformism and misunderstood over the centuries.

The riddle in question is the reference to the number of the beast in Revelations. It is a riddle because for so many centuries, a clear, unequivocal, rationally explainable meaning has remained elusive.

All sorts of strange and unbelievable theories have sprung from this reference but none make any sense, at least in terms of guiding peoples' behaviour.

So, in short, I have used the practical thinking techniques of modern zetetics to find the answer — an answer that makes sense with reference to other biblical scriptures, that makes sense in rational terms and fits perfectly well with our cultural values, particularly key cultural values that have come from the ancient scriptures themselves.

The biblical caution to 'Beware the Number of the Beast' resonates with meaning at a deep gut level. It has always been a powerful attention grabber because of this but despite its prominence, the true meaning has long remained a mystery.

Always fascinated by this riddle, not long after I began to explore zetetics I decided to apply it to the problem and discovered the hidden truth. The answer was straightforward and very pertinent. Zetetics had revealed the answer to an age-old riddle that was pertinent even to zetetics itself.

In deference to the many thinkers who have failed in their attempt to address this puzzle, it has to be said that confusion in this matter is understandable.

Typically, the initial response might be to ask: how can you beware of a number? It has no strength or power. This, at the very outset, is plainly where most people get lost and cease to consider the matter.

So, the zetetic process begins, employing the specification of finding at least three alternative answers at each stage.

The premise is that we have 'the beast' represented by a number. We wish to know what it is and why a number represents it.

So, what is it?

Context indicates little about it. It could perhaps be a physical creature, a magical being or a concept — maybe a behavioural trait or a way of doing something.

Why does a number represent it?

Given that the meaning is the key issue, what meaning can a number have? So, the minimum of three alternative answers follows.

It could be a name, an identifying mark or some sort of secret code. A number makes a poor name and as an identifying mark, the information it conveys would be insufficiently informative to avoid confusion. Where a number is used beyond the context of simple quantity, it seems likely to indicate a reference to an abstract concept, so the reference is likely to be a code.

Why would the writer use a code?

It could have been intended to stir curiosity, it could have been an issue of security and it could have been simply a fun intellectual exercise. Any of these elements would do but riddles seem to be most aptly geared towards stimulating intellectual curiosity.

What is special, then, about curiosity?

It renews interest in life, it can be dangerous and it is an impetus to the process of knowing. Intellect is a key aspect of spirituality and the book the riddle comes from concerns spirituality, not to mention knowing, (the fruit of the Tree of Knowledge is central to its mandate) so it probably concerns the process of knowing. Knowing is also 'having the eyes to see' that we have been told is central to anavah or what god thinks we should do.

So, what is the process of knowing?

The Three Phases of Knowing (3)
    1 ... Presumption, or the immediate perceptions of something through seeing its most visible external characteristics.
    2 ... Doubt, raised by the perception of new and sometimes seemingly incompatible factors, can lead to confusion and rejection of the thing being considered. It is an essential part of the thinking process but people often simply assume that it only means raising an objection to something that is then held up as certain without further exploration.
    3 ... Resolution of these sometimes seemingly disparate elements through consciously assessing any doubts that might have been raised, leads to the full functional understanding of something, in other words truly knowing what it is.

If the proper processes of mental resolution fail and the mind remains stuck in doubt, the way is paved for terrible indecisiveness, inaction and great evil.

Interestingly, this concept also exists in ancient Chinese philosophy.

Taoism explains the same process in the aphorism of the three stages of perception of the tree, the river and the mountain. First, they seem to be so then they seem not so and finally after careful examination they are known to be so — (but known to be so with a more complex understanding of their reality).

Knowing in this complete, thorough way can relate to the physical, the emotional or the intellectual. It can therefore be sensory perception, emotional clarity or intellectual discovery. In a way, the process of knowing involves them all. More importantly, it has three phases — initial perception, doubt and resolution. These are also the three phases of intellect in Mindcraft.

It is seeing the obvious aspects of things, experiencing doubt when confronted with the hidden or less easily understood aspects of them and finally resolving all the revealed elements into a well-integrated pattern of understanding. Knowing is all these three things in three stages so there may be extra significance in the presence of three stages.

What relationship does the number 666 have to three stages?

It has three numerals (significant perhaps because there are three stages in knowing), the numbers involve repetition, and finally the number represents two-thirds in decimal terms.

Where stages are being considered, and we have already concluded the riddle is most likely about the process of knowing, which has three stages, the meaning of two thirds would be most pertinent.

Which stage out of the first, the second or the third would be most significant?

The second stage is an obvious choice because two thirds is equivalent to the second stage out of three, so the number 666 would most likely relate to the second stage of knowing, in which doubt, or seeing things that are difficult to accept in the context of the initial perception, is characteristically present.

We are told in the ancient text to beware this number so we must consider what great and terrible dangers there could be for us in doubt.

Simply being ignorant and ill-equipped would be hazardous, perhaps also leading to inaction when action would be required. Doubt would also promote unjust rejection through misunderstanding.

Actually, all these things are relevant to us and incredibly dangerous — certainly all things of which we should beware. Failure to know things properly can lead to some very poor choices. Failure to act can lead to disappointment, regret and a free rein for evil. Rejection can lead to ignorance, sadness and conflict. Moreover, all these manifestations of the failure to know can become self-fulfilling vicious circles.

What then are the wider effects of entrenched ignorance, inaction and rejection on a cultural level?

Unfortunately, under their influence, people can actually start to fight to maintain them and they become points of pride. That is how negative societies spawn holy cows. Ill-considered actions statements and conclusions will abound.

There it is. Without going any further, the answer to the initial question at the outset of the process is now very clear. The 'beast' is revealed as a mental flaw — the failure to work through the doubt that assails people after their first perceptions are called into question — a failure that can lead all too easily to the establishment of that most insidious state of ignorance, the worship of holy cows.

As a matter of curious, random co-incidence, we also commonly refer to cows as beasts so we could also call it the number of the holy cow.

The number 666 is the decimal equivalent of two thirds and the zetetically derived conclusion is that it signifies the danger of becoming stuck in the second of the three stages of knowing, the stage of doubt — which we frequently do.

It is clear that the biblical exhortation addresses this second and most problematic stage of the intellectual process, which as it happens most organized religions exploit ruthlessly. The numerology of the Hebrews dictates that 1000 means perfection. If 666 is in fact two-thirds of 1000, it at least means substantially less than perfect and if the concept of the final best possible answer can be viewed as a form of perfection, then anything less must be seen as imperfect or unresolved — therefore a manifestation of doubt.

Hebrew culture says 666 is man's number because that is the way he mostly lives. Only the very ignorant would be unaware of the vast potential for evil unleashed by the loose cannon of the human mind and there can be no doubt that the mythical 'beast' is a graphic image for the human mind run amok.

Organized religions have promulgated many wayward evils with their erratic, unclear thinking and conformist values over the centuries. They rely on misunderstanding because when people fail to understand things they do not know them.

What can breed fear better than anything else? The failure to know or understand something, just as being unable to understand someone's language will promote unreasonable fear of them.

So, this mythical number of the beast has been used over the years by clerical figures to breed fear in their followers.

Revelations has such a wealth of strange and bizarre imagery that it lent itself very well to creating awe and fear, and therefore conformism in parish populations. Beware the number of the beast!

For centuries, it had people looking all over the place for things that should not be done or should be avoided for fear of eternal damnation. Who knows, Revelations and its Number of the Beast and Mark of the Beast may even have caused the appalling, cruel and disgusting Witch Craze.

Confused and wayward church followers found themselves doing exactly the sort of thing that the warning had, with the proper interpretation, intended to prevent them from doing.

This sort of thing could only come from organized religions who had a material interest in promoting both fear and conformism.

That the riddle of the Number of the Beast refers to the processes of thought run amok is very clear but it is also supported by other high-profile biblical stories with similar themes — most specifically the mystic fruit of temptation in the Garden of Eden, portrayed by Milton as an apple in Paradise Lost, which organized religion has used to impose guilt on people as a permanent burden.

A more enlightened, logical and constructive view of the story would see it as a symbolic representation of the need to explore beyond the immediate perceptions of things or the perceptions that others plant in our minds, as the serpent did with Eve.

After all, the fruit does come from the Tree of Knowledge of Good and Evil and perception is relevant because it is the first stage of knowing.

God, in the Hebrew writings, if that's who he is, is clearly very concerned about the issue of knowledge and perception but he cannot have wanted people not to know things. All sentient creatures know things and God gave us senses with which to know things so any problem that he perceives cannot be with humanity knowing but rather with humanity not knowing properly.

Zetetic interpretation of the 'number of the beast' story says that it is not immediate perception that is the problem. It is the second stage that people most easily become hung up on — after things present as different to what they originally seemed to be.

Given that, ancient, divinely inspired thinkers might well have felt that the matter of knowing was crucial and needed to be properly understood.

In this parable, the doubt stage was addressed when the serpent drew the attention of Eve to the fruit and made her wonder about what they really were.

So, did Eve resolve this doubt or not?

Apparently not, and if she did not then it would be no surprise if she was led into fear, guilt and confusion. If she went into a decision to eat the fruit simply on the advice of the serpent without actually considering the matter, herself, then the negative, evil results would be entirely consistent with what we would expect from our understanding of the 'number of the beast' riddle. The fruit would be associated with evil, not because it was innately evil but because what it represented was poorly understood and because Adam and Eve did not look to understanding its significance.

After all, god gave us the capability of logic and beyond any contention, if we fail to use it then we open ourselves up to evil and suffering even in the face of the best he can offer us — the pure, sweet and wholesome fruit from the Tree of Knowledge of Good and Evil.

Yes, it seems clear that the fruit itself was not really the problem! Perhaps on one level, it was a symbolic representation of the idea that not everything is as it appears to be but primarily it is a parable about looking before you leap and very carefully using your own judgment.

When we realize that the writer, whether it was God or not, intended us to see the possibilities of knowledge through reasoning and run with it, we are led to a much more kindly and beneficent view of the divine and the Fruit of the Tree of Knowledge of Good and Evil becomes a good and wholesome thing — an impetus to knowing and in fact the greatest gift any god could ever bestow upon us. It clearly means that God wishes us to ask questions; to look before we leap — in clear accordance with the principle of anavah.

Religion has taught us to fear knowledge but the ancient scriptures intended for us to use it effectively through being aware of the primary pitfalls of life. One common saying that fits the bill very well here is 'a little knowledge is a dangerous thing'.

On another level, earlier mentioned, the story is about free will. The fact that Adam and Eve could no longer live in paradise after eating the fruit and became more conscious is simply a natural consequence of their growth as individuals. My brother, Mark, pointed out to me that the forbidden fruit tree was placed centrally in the garden and that some scholars believe that this meant it symbolized the most central part of our nervous system

— the brain. It meant that eating the fruit was like using the brain in a way that is not purely sensory.

And indeed, how could they grow or become more aware in a place where there were no challenges?

Adam and Eve's new consciousness of their nakedness had to be a metaphor for their increasing conscious awareness. Given that they were already aware in some ways, the metaphor clearly must indicate a growing level of consciousness — perhaps that desirable generation of consciousness that begins to develop when you use your reasoning capacity.

If this is the case and these were real events, then this God figure must always have intended that Adam and Eve should eat the fruit and our large organized religions have perverted the truth of this story into the dreadful irrevocable covenant of 'original sin' for their own manipulative ends.

The Creation Story: A Misinterpreted Myth

There can be little doubt that the story of Adam and Eve is a myth and the only way that we could perpetuate any evil would be to do what somebody else wanted us to do unquestioningly, as Eve did with the serpent. Look at it logically and you will see that it is a parable — not a covenant.

The serpent told Eve that she and her husband would be like God if they ate the fruit but if religious orthodoxy is right about all this and it really did have some sort of mystical power, God would actually have guarded his power more effectively if his intent was keeping Adam and Eve in their place.

If that was the case or even if the power simply had the potential to corrupt them, there is no way that he would have put them within cooee of the Tree of Knowledge in the first place.

Thus, the serpent's lie that they could be like God and that God was trying (oh yes, so effectively) to guard against that happening was pretty weak and anyone would have seen that if they had stopped to think about it for more than two seconds.

If in truth, God told them that they would die if they ate the fruit, and if indeed Adam and Eve as yet had no true capacity to know the nuances and implications of good and evil, he could not have made it totally clear to them what death was. If this was the case, and eating the fruit was truly the source of 'original sin' then God would hardly have been playing fair. He would have been warning people who had no properly developed capacity to understand the warning. The religious rendition of this myth is a completely circular fallacy. Adam and Eve had no way out.

Clearly, the proper rendition of the story, unaltered by the all too likely deception of organized religion meddlers, would have been somewhat different. Instead, God might have warned them that great change would come from eating the fruit from the Tree of Knowledge of Good and Evil and that they should not do so lightly, especially on the advice of someone else.

Reaching new stages of awareness can be difficult, as with children reaching puberty. Ceasing to be what they were could be interpreted as a sort of death. Once you're an adult the child is gone. Tarot cards of death are usually interpreted this way, for instance. So, God might have warned them that they would cease to be what they were: largely unaware, incomplete beings only in the early stages of what he intended them to be — like children in fact.

The next step in their development would be difficult, as being an adult is, so apparently God deemed it better left in their hands as to when they would take that step, given that the Tree of Knowledge was in easy reach of them within the garden.

Given the fact that how and when we enter phases of significant change can greatly affect how we experience them, for better or worse, it would probably be better if we do not institute such changes on the advice of other people, as Eve did.

Just as God warned Adam and Eve of this challenging potential for great change, we might well tell a child who is playing with matches that he will burn himself. Most children would find out pretty quickly then what 'burn' means but the consequences would only be a sore finger for a few hours — not the end of paradise with eternal guilt and no silver lining.

So, what sort of a god would punish people with a burden like 'original sin' for doing what he must always have intended them to do?

No, the true lesson of this myth has to be that if you are to make the best choices in a world of many good and evil potentials, you will be much better off not blindly accepting the influence of others and instead using your God given reasoning skills to carefully assess every situation as it comes up.

This in turn ties in beautifully with the Norse myths about Idunn's golden apples that endow eternal life — for what could better provide us the means to attain eternal life than the growth of consciousness and responsibility?

Moreover, it was said that people should eat these magical apples on a regular basis — just as the magic of conscious awareness can be enhanced through will in each and every moment.

The symbolic representation of these biblical stories is a crucial part of promoting abstract thought processes.

Such a method of expression would be perfectly fit for task where the intent was to stimulate awareness of key issues concerning intellectual function.

Given the current state of the world and its history, it is no wonder that ancient mystics felt the need to draw attention to such concepts.

In the modern world, the concept revealed in the temptation story is still amazingly relevant. Churches, large corporations and corrupt politicians take advantage of a lack of critical thinking in people to impose ever-greater spiritually destructive conformity and compassionless domination on them.

The chaos that this conformity generates leaves an ever-increasing trail of pain and destruction in its wake that these corrupt forces further use to impose still more conformity and domination. Those are the wages of sin, which as it happens means 'to miss the mark' or, if you want me to be even clearer, 'miss the point'.

Why did Jesus advise us to pray in private specifically behind closed doors if he did not want us having a direct relationship with God that involved praying directly, unmediated, to him? His words in the Sermon on the Mount are clearly aimed at forming a private relationship with God.

In the light of this understanding of the private nature of religion, we should abandon the division created by dogma and unite under a code of social behaviour designed to draw out the best of intellectual, emotional and spiritual characteristics in people.

Doing this, we could cast aside confusion and bring together all our great strengths to order the world in ways that its original creator would be proud to see.

The cultivation of a new coherent social code based in a comprehensive spiritual understanding is of vital and central importance. It will be essential to breaking the downward spiral of awareness that all these bizarre shades of the past have caused.

Chapter 19 — Leadership Succession

The urgent need for a new kind of leadership is beyond question. A new and carefully constructed version of a monarchic system offers the not inconsiderable benefit of reference to a long and largely successful set of traditions throughout the world.

Also, the undeniable merit of placing final responsibility for decisions in one pair of hands facilitates conscious cogitation, deliberate choice and responsibility over expediency, corruption and irresponsibility.

Good leadership needs to maintain and own responsibility for its decisions far beyond any typical elected term of office. It needs a sense of belonging, lifelong preparation, the proper appreciation of honour and a sense of familial care.

Some of these things might occasionally manifest in elected leaders but any just, considerate leader can so easily be followed by a bad one, undoing all the good works of his predecessor. His responsibility for that destruction then lasts only as long as his office.

Beyond that, a want of personal wealth might open a leader to influence by corrupt forces. For that reason, a generous income should be awarded to a monarch, a fair fraction of which he could keep even if removed.

The merits of monarchy have been discussed at length already and while I do not wish to be repetitive, I stand ready to justify it over any other system.

Yet even this preferred system cannot continue to operate effectively without a carefully considered and structured system of leadership succession. In the past, particularly in Britain, the dearth of royal heirs let alone suitable ones led to some horrific instabilities and wars. It caused the deaths and suffering of many and in large part this was caused in turn by the stupid constraints of the religious powers of the time.

One queen might produce only one heir and at times even none at all. Limiting, monogamous relationships artificially imposed on communities by hypocritical and inconsistent religious laws led to a shortage of heirs but even had there been more, the same insane religious influence would have dictated that the firstborn alone had the chance to be king. That firstborn might not be the best candidate or even a good one but he would be imposed on the people anyway.

A more sensible and constructive system would allow a king multiple wives and would dictate that each son of qualifying age could compete for the office upon the death of the king or in the unlikely event of his discharge for reasons of incompetence.

If the first king in such a system was discharged by noble vote on an allowable charge of incompetence and he had no sons of qualifying age or even if he had less than say, three sons of qualifying age, then other high-ranking nobles could contend. The need for a wide choice of strong contenders would outweigh loyalty to the king's house until sufficient contenders could be provided by that house.

Given that this monarchy would be the first and unproven, its status would be provisional and highly dependent on performance. Gradually, over time and with proven successes, a royal house could well attract greater loyalty and greater rights of continuance. Even so, an unjust or incompetent king could be removed and a successor chosen from his heirs.

So, given the importance of stability in such a system, just how could a monarch be removed?

In such a system, a comprehensive bill of human rights, monarchic powers and processes of selection would have to be drafted and enacted by the noble court before a king was chosen from amongst them. All would agree to be bound by those conditions and requirements, which would include all those rights enjoyed by the most advanced of democracies but enforced and protected by the will of the noble house and one ultimately responsible mind.

With the act of decision ultimately in one set of hands, those decisions could be weighed and assessed more easily and accurately. The buck could not be passed and if there was a need to, the will of a monarch could be more effectively challenged than the will of a group of decision makers such as cabinet or parliament.

Once a vote has been taken in a democratic house, no one needs to stand ready to be accountable for it. The decision stands solely because of the vote numbers rather because of any reasonable justification for it and even if circumstances change, it typically takes a long time for a parliament to get back to the decision and review it. A monarch could press through a review if his conscience or sense of peoples' needs gave it weight.

A good monarch would know as well as anyone what was needed but would also have the ear of those who could make it happen. Normal people are often burdened with a host of difficult problems of a basic nature which prevent them coming up with plans and strategies for broader social issues and they rarely have the time or the energy to listen to the needs of others let alone do anything about them.

So, with all the current world leaders running around in circles, fighting with each other and ignoring the real problems, a king or emperor with real power could do something radical.

Our democratic leaders are killing our oceans and rivers, polluting our air, degrading our food, destroying the land and destroying our mental and physical health but a true monarch could order things largely according to his single vision, so long as it was constructive and positive.

It has been clear to me for some time that our supposed democracies in the west are a complete farce and that the only way we can get anything done is by having a true leader — a leader for life who has his heart and soul invested in doing the right thing because he can and because doing the right thing fits with the identity/role he has in the world.

So, in the end we need to proclaim a king of the world — an emperor in fact. You can frown on the idea or you can applaud it but the fact is we need one and no one is going to simply get voted in as leader of the world. Our democracies would never allow it. No one is going to take the role by force either. No one can be born into it but if Jesus did come back, one presumes he would have the power to force the issue.

The fact is, we need a worldwide federation with the power to institute a leader. We need one unifying language, at least for the purpose of government and trade, and a clear, constructive moral code.

No one nation can drive the development of that. It can only happen through an enduring international cooperation driven by individuals with the vision and the guts to stick by what they believe in, drawing on the resources of all the great nations.

Many people are confused by having to make important decisions and simply do not want to. In all honesty they want to be looked after and it is clear that neither capitalist democracy nor communism have effectively done so.

Only a sufficiently large groundswell can generate the political momentum required to achieve the sorts of worldwide goals that will ultimately be necessary. There needs to be a 'smart league' to drive a 'smart revolution' because in the end it is smart to be safe and happy.

So, if the movement was successful and the time came for a leader to be chosen, what basic criteria would our organization use to choose such a man? I imagine this point might be well-debated but it seems clear that each candidate would need to be measured against the others by a number of means to determine relative levels of admirable and worthy qualities.

The qualities that could hardly be left out from this list would be:

Wisdom
Independent Intelligence
Emotional Intelligence
Honour
Compassion
Courage
Lucid communication abilities
Cleverness
Health
Strength

The means by which this would be assessed would be:

Reference to previous activities
Situational contest
Problem solving
Monitoring of conduct between competitors
Informal debates over meals
Situational coping with new skills
Situational coping with physical risk
Written reactions to hypotheticals

Game contests
Medical assessment
Individual physical sports contests

I believe it's important to note that the choice would not necessarily be made of the person with the highest overall score but that reasonable ability in these things would be a prerequisite and the final choice would be made predominantly from the candidates' personal insight and vision.

In the wake of such comprehensive assessments of character, strength, intellect and responsiveness, I believe that a leader would be chosen who was of a far superior calibre to anyone yet chosen for leadership. Presidential candidates do not undergo such comprehensive and intense scrutiny nor do Prime Ministerial ones.

In fact, such people have never before been required to prove by any particular capabilities they might have to lead effectively and compassionately. Is it any wonder then that we have had such poor leadership to date?

It is my sincere hope that greater awareness of the issues raised in this work will inspire the formation and growth of a global organization capable of generating the will to take up the fight for just, effective and compassionate leadership.

Adequate action has long been wanting and a new brotherhood is needed to wrest control from the criminals that have dominated the world's affairs for so long.

The fact is, in our modern world of horrors, we no longer have the time to quibble over candles when only a lasting source of illumination will suffice.

Conclusion: The Threat

In the introduction of this work I presented a bare outline of the dangers we face by remaining with the current system of government and outlined the basic reasons why monarchic feudalism is the only practical alternative for rule in a world faced with so many dire threats. The basic instrument of feudal monarchy worked quite well for many thousands of years but yes, it could always have worked better and with the right evolutionary changes it could work vastly better in the future.

This is the bullet point list reiterated from my introduction (21 elements) of what we will endure if we fail to face reality and institute effective change:

- fiscal and economic servitude
- loss of freedoms to do and think reasonable things
- loss of a sense of fun and delight in living
- loss of rights during pandemics and other emergencies
- the spread of confusion and hypocrisy
- accelerating environmental degradation
- loss of a sense of the importance of truth and of beauty
- extra dangers inherent in coercive regimes leading to such things as research into bio weapons and other vehicles of social control
- directionless leadership governed by the lowest factors of expediency
- indecision because of equality of power amongst decision making representatives
- irresponsibility inherent in temporary leaders
- hunger and disease both mental and physical
- allowing poor criteria for choosing leaders because they are only temporary
- bad decisions from the absence of a truly spiritual code
- giving lowest elements the freedom to behave dishonourably
- giving criminals the reins of power
- societies governed by fear

- periodic war and destruction
- bloodthirsty Bolshevik style revolutions and chaos
- increasing degradation in the worst forms of slavery
- possible destruction of all higher forms of life on the planet

The fact is, to avoid the cataclysm resulting from the combined effect of the above elements, there are no other alternatives than adopting a clear architecture for decisive, improving long-term rule.

Communism has failed but has created accelerating chaos in attempting to sabotage western societies from within. Democratic representatives have fallen under the veiled spell of communism and lumber along letting the communists get away with murder and even doing some of their foul work for them.

White Caucasian people vary more in their intelligence, with the top few percent being geniuses who top the world and where other powerful races have a more homogenous intelligence, democracy and communism might suit them but does not suit us. If we champion democracy, we pander to the less intelligent and capable amongst us and deny the astonishing excellence of our top-ranking people. In other words, we stack the odds against ourselves.

Good leadership is the miracle we need and I have specified in these chapters just what it would take to bring about this lost ideal of good leadership, including a properly integrated form of monarchy, nobility governed by core principles of communication, compassion and reason and the majority of people returning to producing their own quality basics of life — especially food.

Monarchic feudalism can and will work well but if it is to do so effectively, we must ensure that it cannot be sabotaged in any way by other unsympathetic elements in the way that our societies recently have been.

The best way to ensure that sabotage does not occur would be to specify that the new system espouses a clear and effective spiritual code and that those who govern through this new system are carefully trained in the complete understanding of it.

This will help our leaders more easily identify what is not in keeping with the code or with justice (the right way) Elements of the code, such as meditation have a good track record of increasing intelligence, which will also help people to identify incongruous elements or propositions.

We must have a capable nobility who believe completely in the power and justice of the code and who will have a life-long loyalty to the cause of caring for society as a whole.

Every individual in society would ultimately have a purpose and be aided in the fulfilment of that purpose by the emperor and the nobles but we cannot get there without first having a core group who will lead us in the construction and implementation of this new system.

The old system of monarchy may have failed us in the past or even our recent past, best exemplified by the British monarchy that said and did nothing to oppose the recent callous abuse of human rights, but it ruled best for longest and a similar system could be protected from failure in a number of critical ways.

Also, we have to acknowledge that the most spectacular failures of monarchy were driven by sustained attack from communist forces.

We need to see things as they really are and recognize the truth about these historical attacks or we will remain blind to what was good in the past and blind to any similar threats in the future. Few are students of history now so few will know that committed, focused antagonistic forces have been working in concert to undermining us for some time.

Communism has been rearing its ugly head for many generations now, starting in some ways as early as the French Revolution but quickly progressing to become more globally organized and insidious.

Both the proponents of and the initial effects of communism remain largely unseen. The change is gradual but always in the direction of less rights, benefits and fulfilment for the individual.

From a general perspective, life for the majority of people in western societies has become a chore rather than an adventure in fulfilment featuring unique pleasures along the way.

Such negative changes have filtered in because amoral communist elements are hard at work subverting government administration and undermining family life with their 'progressive' policies like legalizing abortion for any reason, reducing parental governance, promoting sexual promiscuity and goading women into the workforce whether they really want it or not.

On top of that, like the black icing on the cake, they undermine the educational environment for boys in every way they can and drive the deep suspicion that accompanies the Me-Too movement.

These subversive elements then promote racial integration in white societies when most other major societies — Japan, China, Korea, Israel, Russia and the like do not want a bar of it.

I personally do not like the goal of racial integration but there is no cause to be unreasonable. If a mixed-race pair wants to marry they should not be vilified but neither can they be allowed to hold any prominent position in a society trying to preserve its genetic heritage. When virtually all our advertising, our fashion industry, our movies and our media continually bombard our young people with charming, happy, attractive mixed-race images, surely we must ask why!

At the same time, the modern portrayal of the typical white western male in Hollywood movies is that he is either a terrible villain or an unprincipled slob.

Most of these communist policies are, oddly enough, secretly dictated by banks — the policies that destroy forests and old buildings, that bring down regimes and fund new communist ones, that build in basic flaws to manufactured products, that make governments coercive, that make businesses pursue unjust, dictatorial practises, that promote war and have doctors undermining health instead of repairing it.

Everything is either about generating more money or cementing control rather than about serving human interests — and behind it all, covertly, are those who control the banking and finance industries.

I've seen that our schools have grown more and more along the lines of telling the children what to do rather than helping them discover what they want to do. I've seen them push the spirit of conformism on young minds like they never did in my time and the poor youngsters are too afraid to express themselves.

I've seen that government, at least here in Australia, is growing accustomed to pushing people around more and more, forcing vaccinations on the poor and the workers with their 'no jab no pay' welfare support payments and with the astonishing proliferation of regulations — so many thousands of rules about which most of the population is completely ignorant.

I've seen that businesses increasingly have the attitude that they are right — not the customer and that you should bloody well be glad to accept their service no matter how bad it is.

I've seen people look at me strangely when I tell them that the fruit tastes flavourless nowadays — like pears were meant to be all like wood and apricots were meant to be pink flavourless mush — like apples were meant to have thick, tough skins and oranges were meant to be all dry and shrivelled inside. And if I do not like it, then I should simply just not buy it? But there's nothing else available!

The trouble is, it is not simply the basic, utilitarian things that have suffered. We have also lost much of the magic in life. People are bored and afraid and, now, worst of all cowed. Increasingly, they are accepting that they should just do what they are told.

This is no way for people to live and it is all because the communists keep telling us by one means or another that the individual does not matter. Their excuse is that the group outlasts the individual so it matters more despite the fact that it does not have a mind, a heart or a soul, but in truth the group suffers as well and only the leadership benefits.

More than anything else, communism is about convincing people that the group is more important than the individual. That is the vile beast's essence and you will know that something or someone is communist if it fails that test. If the group outweighs the individual, then communism is there, growing like toxic mould.

My father used to get impatient with me when I called some conservative party hack (someone who in the USA would now be called a Republican In Name Only) a communist — but he failed to understand just how far the ugly rot had crept into society. Communism is a state of mind, not a brand and you have to call it where you see it.

Personally, I witnessed this sort of behaviour while operating as a skipper in the New South Wales volunteer ocean rescue organization, MRNSW, and learned that despite a profusion of rules and regulations in place supposedly designed to make things fair and put a brake on the wayward wrecking balls of senior hierarchy, it was all completely ineffective in the end.

A more destructive, dishonest, immoral, poorly trained organization you could not get, wherein incompetent morons are promoted and good people are slapped around before being thrown out.

That is it, people. If you live in a modern western style democracy, it will have the appearance of a free democracy but when push comes to shove, you will in the end be forced to face the truth — that it is actually communist authoritarianism in disguise.

It was not like that nearly so much in the past but things have changed. Communism has come upon us by stealth and now, unless we strive with all our strength and ingenuity against it, it will be here to stay and our children and their children will be slaves.

Which sounds better? Living under the rule of a monarch who can make considered, conscious decisions with reference to his individual vision and who cares about the individual — or living under the thumb of communist bank-controlled puppet bureaucracies that forever generate more rules?

It is no secret that the highest aims of the greatest minds in human history have not only been to expand the potentials of their understanding of the external world but also to push back the frontiers of the inner human experience and to cast light on the shadows no matter what they may be.

It is also no secret that the revelations of inner truth are often sacrificed, in our modern society, to the needy demands of political expediency.

Compromise has long been one of the key arts of survival in this world but the storm that is coming has no parallel. I don't believe we have ever experienced the like of what is coming. The challenges and suffering will likely be cruel in the extreme.

Finding the best way forward requires a completely different approach and if we take it, instead of widespread suffering, there will be huge gains in material, social and spiritual terms.

So, finally, if you do nothing, you get the absolute entrenchment of an oligarchy of wealth that already exists, handing power to the worst sort of people devoid of imagination and family spirit, who will treat you and the planet worse than nine tenths of the kings ever did.

If you do work for change, you can realistically hope for a system that installs the best sort of men, outstanding in a variety of ways, to make the greater decisions that have so far been studiously avoided or entirely ignored — decisions that are vital to our survival on this planet into the future.

Epilogue — The Bolshevik Threat

Many people cite Russia's experience with communism as an argument for watching its influence more closely and opposing it. It certainly created an epoch of murder and mayhem like no other and it was essentially an invasion by external forces including individuals from several countries other than Russia — and from people of a very different culture.

In past centuries, many European Jews entered Russia for one reason or another. Jews had been accepted into Russia from Poland and elsewhere in large numbers in the spirit of tolerance. They had also been accepted from the middle east because Moslems were said to be persecuting them there. There were around five million of them in Russia before the Great War but they ended up being restricted in various ways including travel within the realm for a number of alleged reasons.

If all the historical accusations against them were true, it would not have been surprising if they had been ejected but in fact the czars did not deport them.

Yet by the time of Alexander the Second's rule in Russia, coherent communist elements that included some hard-line Jews were becoming very disciplined and well-organized in attacking the establishment.

An attack by quasi-communist elements in 1881 changed everything. Tzar Alexander II was killed when the Narodnaya Volya bombed his carriage on the streets of St Petersburg and in a supremely ironical twist of fate, on the very day he was killed, he had signed a brave historic proclamation instituting a new liberal constitution that would have created two legislative commissions comprising indirectly elected representatives.

Tzar Alexander II had done much to liberalize and modernize Russia but his murder led his son, Alexander III to rescind many of those advances.

Strangely, considering his upper middle-class family background, Vladimir Lenin's elder brother Aleksandr Ilyich Ulyanov became a revolutionary. His parents were upper middle-class monarchists but he was part Jewish. After joining the Narodnaya Volya, he plotted with them to murder the Tzar on the sixth anniversary of Tzar Alexander II's murder, with a bomb containing strychnine laced lead pellets.

The plot was discovered and some of the conspirators, including Ulyanov, who was also the bomb-maker, were hanged. After this and after his father's death from a brain bleed, Vladimir Lenin's revolutionary activities appeared to step up. This is amazing because if the Czarist rule was so autocratic, why was Ulyanov's part Jewish brother not immediately placed under close watch or even incarcerated?

According to Wikipedia, Vladimir as a child was inclined to boss his younger sister Olga around and could be quite destructive around the house. Later, in 1903, as a key member of the Russian communist party the RSDLP, he advocated that ordinary party members should not be allowed to express themselves independent of the leadership.

In this he was opposed by Martov, who advocated the opposite, that party members should be allowed to express themselves. The majority of these revolutionaries supported Lenin and the name Bolshevik was coined because it meant the majority. Martov's group were called Mensheviks because they were in the minority and that name meant the minority.

Arrested in the end for seditious activities several times, Vladimir Lenin was exiled for three years in 1897 to a peasant village in central Siberia. While there, he lived in a peasant's hut, was allowed to write letters, have visitors, was permitted to go swimming in the river as well as go hunting and fishing!

During that time his girlfriend came to stay with him and they got married. Sounds more like a country holiday than prison to me. When the exile was over, he was permitted to return to the city and take his final exam to become a lawyer.

By comparison, when Lenin took over the rule of Russia yes, he did exile the Tzar and his family but they were not allowed to leave the house and go swimming in the river, and were eventually murdered en-masse in cold blood. What a terrible man Lenin was — bossy, vindictive, destructive, authoritarian and cruel.

Alexander III ruled under increasing pressure from just these sorts of revolutionaries and died relatively young leaving an also relatively young and inexperienced Nicholas II to contend with steadily increasing levels of communist sabotage and infiltration.

At the same time, the banking world refused to lend to Russia to help it properly equip its military ahead of the war with Japan. Indeed, the banks funded Japan instead. Much the same sort of thing happened with funding in World War One. Meanwhile, Britain provided advanced weaponry to Japan that gave them a huge advantage over the Russians.

Furthermore, in that war, started primarily by Austria, German communist elements undermined Russian leadership and society. Britain was supposedly Russia's ally but consistently failed to give sufficient aid when it was desperately needed.

Communist elements regularly sabotaged an already beleaguered army, suffering terrible shortages of supplies and equipment, and steadily worked to turn the ordinary soldiers against their leaders at times of crisis in their inevitable defeats.

After Tzar Nicholas II abdicated, a short period of limited positive reform took place under the Provisional Government but Kerensky's decision to continue fighting the war and his mismanagement of the Kornilov affair weakened it to the point of collapse. In the face of this weakness, the Bolsheviks' consistent decisiveness in adopting extreme measures in their activism gained them strong support from the simplest and most disaffected elements of Russian society.

The extremist authoritarian Bolsheviks took advantage of simple workers in factory committees, promising them greater economic freedom and using them to seize power from the Provisional Government in the 1917 October revolution. The human consequences that followed from this opportunistic and clearly deceitful grab for power were catastrophic.

Millions of Russians died in the blood-letting of Bolshevik consolidation of power and untold millions more, including many of the workers who had supported them, were murdered by the Bolsheviks once their grip on power was complete.

It has been said that Czarist Russia took advantage of the sweat of other peoples' brows but prior to the Great War and the subsequent depredations of the Bolsheviks, life for most Russians was relatively comfortable and secure, as indicated by the liberal manner in which Vladimir Lenin was punished for sedition.

If you were to compare being a serf on a well-run noble's property to being a proletariat citizen under the Bolsheviks or even to being a poorly paid modern wage slave in a job you hate while being in debt to banks ready to foreclose on you at the drop of a hat, such a life would probably seem wonderful.

Early in the 20th century, communism grew fast and behind it was the Bolshevik core that ended up in the Russian 1917 Narrow Composition, the highest policy-making authority within the Communist Party of the Soviet Union.

There were seven men in that initial key group of emergency decision-makers later known as the Political Bureau. They held sway over the Sovnarkom, which forcefully took over from the Underground Provisional Government in the wake of the October Revolution. The initial members were Vladimir Lenin, Leon Trotsky, Grigori Zinoviev, Lev Kamenev, Joseph Stalin, Grigori Sokolnikov and Andrei Bubnov.

Only two had no Jewish blood — Stalin and Bubnov — and Stalin was from Georgia, in the general region from where the dominant Ashkenazy Jews came. Lenin was one eighth Jewish from his maternal grandfather.

Lenin was born in Russia but his mother was German, Swedish and Jewish in background. Trotsky was a Jew born in Ukraine who had earlier been one of the Narodniki. Zinoviev was a Jew born in Ukraine. Kamenev was Russian but Jewish and his parents were also revolutionaries. Stalin was from Georgia. Grigori Sokolnikov was a Ukrainian Jew whose real name was Girsh Yankelevich Brilliant and Bubnov was Russian.

Thus, only Bubnov was truly Russian and the rule of the Political Bureau can justifiably be seen as a foreign takeover.

David Duke tells us in My Awakening that Leon Trotsky (real name Lev Bronstein) in his book, 'Stalin', claimed that Stalin was quite insignificant in the early days. He reproduced a postcard showing the then six leaders of the revolution. They were part Jewish and native Yiddish speaker Lenin, Trotsky, Jewish Zinoviev (real name Hirsch Apfelbaum), Gentile Anatoly Lunacharsky, Jewish Kamanev (real name Rosenfeld) and Jewish Sverdlov.

One out of six, Lunacharsky, was not Jewish but he was Ukrainian by birth, not Russian. Nor was he a very powerful figure in the leadership, spoken of by others in the leadership scornfully and kept away from high decision making. More a man of culture, he did contribute to the preservation and promotion of culture in post revolutionary Russia.

Duke also tells of a table made up in 1918 by Robert Wilton, Russian correspondent for the highly influential 'London Times', showing the composition of the extremely powerful and ruthless commissars. There were 384 and of those 384, 13 were Russian and more than 300 were Jews. US Army intelligence reported the ghastly massacre of thousands of Russian nobles and intelligentsia, simply because they were potential leaders against the Bolshevik communists but this was only the start. It is well known that many millions died in the early days under the leadership of Lenin and Trotsky, well before Stalin gained supremacy.

Under the subsequent maelstrom of Bolshevik rule, heavily funded by the mega rich Jew, Jacob Schiff, many tens of millions of Russians and Ukrainians died of starvation or were killed until Stalin eventually wrested power from the others by sheer chicanery and bloodthirsty butchery.

Wikipedia says that somewhere between 28 million and 126 million were killed by the Communist Party of the Soviet Union between 1917 and 1987 but they say a prudent estimate of this number is 61,911,000 — nearly

62 million people. This was the major holocaust of the 20th century and done with unimaginable cruelty.

Basically, the worst of the bloodbath ended with Stalin's demise. He also killed indiscriminately because he had been intent on what he saw as beating his fellow Political Bureau members at their own game.

Over the years since then, the style of Russian leadership has changed dramatically and the influence of unfettered communism has declined.

After the collapse of the Soviet Union, many Jews left Russia, perhaps made unwelcome by an association with hard-line Bolshevism which one must acknowledge in many cases might not have been fair.

So where did they go subsequently?

According to David Duke, they went to the USA and other western nations, which is interesting because most of the 300 or so Jewish commissars had come to Russia from the United States. Some went to Palestine to fight to establish the Israeli state and not all their activities have been universally approved by history.

In Duke's book, 'My Awakening', he describes how armed men killed civilian men, women and children in Palestine and in neighbouring countries like Syria so that they could take over those lands. Rogue elements one supposes, as can exist in any culture.

Yet Duke also wrote about how these Israeli forces tried and very nearly succeeded in destroying the USS Liberty, a USA navy intelligence ship (34 worthy men killed and 170 injured), possibly because the Israelis, who are and were US allies at the time, suspected that the US intelligence operatives aboard Liberty had overheard key communications about the horrific killings of Syrian and Palestinian civilian non-combatants. Clearly, some of the aforementioned rogue elements were high up the leadership ladder.

More recent evidence has come to light in the wake of Donald Trump's second presidential victory which says that senior Israeli figures planned the operation in cahoots with US intelligence services (CIA) a year in advance to set up a reason to take drastic action against Egypt, with whom Israel was at war, a strategy vaguely reminiscent of what happened over Pearl Harbour.

Yet, by this time, Egypt's air-force had already been almost completely destroyed so it would have been difficult to blame Egypt even without witnesses. Even so, for some crazy reason they went ahead with it anyway.

It has to be said that some of the Israeli pilots refused to launch weapons against their close allies and retreated from action but it is said that one who forbore from murdering allies and friends, rather than being praised and promoted, was held and court-martialled in the days following the incident.

The story of the USS Liberty was shocking enough but to then learn that the unelected US President known as LBJ (Lyndon Baines Johnson of part Jewish blood, who had replaced murdered John F Kennedy) called back a flight of US fighters from a nearby carrier before they could intervene because it might 'embarrass their ally', made me feel that something was, and probably still is, very wrong in the American political system.

Eventually, help came from the carriers and the USS Liberty survived. The incident was subject to an investigation but this enquiry was cut very short.

Then comes Richard Nixon, who defeated the unelected part Jewish Johnson heavily in 1969 and was re-elected with a massive vote for his second term before being impeached, largely because of his own poor judgement.

According to Tucker Carlson, in a video piece in March 2025, Nixon believed there were elements in government who had long been working to undermine the American system of government.

On June 23, 1972, Nixon held a conversation with CIA director Richard Helms at the White House. The conversation was recorded and Nixon said that he knew who had 'shot John', meaning John F Kennedy. Nixon further implied that the CIA was directly involved in his assassination. Helms did not respond.

According to Carlson, four days earlier, on June 19, the Washington Post had published the first of numerous stories about a break-in at the Watergate office building. Was Nixon telling Helms about what he knew about JFK to try and gain leverage against the forces he knew were already at work against him or was this just a chance revelation at a routine meeting? Having seen an old recording of a conversation between Billy Graham and President Nixon which revealed much awareness about the state of things, I believe Nixon must have known what was coming.

Carlson went on to assert that four of the five burglars worked for the CIA. Moreover, Bob Woodward, who was one of the principal writers of the Watergate articles, had little background in journalism but had recently been a naval officer at the Pentagon with a Top Secret clearance. Strangely, he jumped from this role to journalism with the Washington Post and, without any extensive news writing experience, was somehow immediately assigned to this massive story. To top it all, his main source was the Deputy Director of the FBI, Mark Felt, who, according to Carlson, ran the Co-Intel-Pro program, which was designed to secretly discredit unwanted political figures, such as Richard Nixon.

When Nixon's VP, Spiro Agnew, was later indicted for tax evasion and forced to resign, Democrats in congress forced Nixon into accepting Gerald Ford as his VP, who had served on the Warren Commission, which had absolved the CIA of any involvement in the murder of President Kennedy. A little down the track, Nixon was out and Ford, of the apparently corrupt Warren Commission was in as an unelected president.

I see no reason to glorify Nixon, who if he was framed by inimical forces, did not react in the way a sensible, clear headed, responsible man would have. The fact that the language in the Oval Office tapes was vulgar and offensive was of less consequence than Nixon's flawed instinct to cover up. David Duke comments on him a number of times in 'My Awakening' in less than glowing terms and if Tucker Carlson achieves anything by his defence of Nixon, it is to draw attention to the fact that powerful elements in US government were involved in the murder of one of their best ever presidents — a president who wanted to see the rule of America returned to its racial core.

Another matter worth quoting from Dr Duke's 'My Awakening' (p 288) is the story of how the Washington Post was taken over for a pittance after people from a particular culture very big in the advertising industry starved it of advertising revenue. The Washington Post had been started in 1877 by Gentile Stilson Hutchins then run by the conservative McLean family but was sent into bankruptcy by the advertising industry. In 1933, Jewish financier Eugene Meyer bought it for next to nothing in receivership. It was still under Jewish ownership at the time of the Watergate affair and purchased by Jeff Bezos in 2013.

I don't know a great deal about USA business culture and laws but if monopolies exist in any form, familial, corporate or cultural that can so gravely affect society as a whole, the issue seems worthy of further investigation. After all, apparently the same thing happened to the other great newspaper of the USA, the New York Times.

In the same vein but rather more significant was the story in Duke's book about how the Rothschilds' fortune was made at the end of the Battle of Waterloo by the then Baron Rothschild misleading the public into believing that Napoleon had won the war and thereby causing a severe stock crash!

Yes, according to Duke, he had a line of small vessels strung across the English Channel to quickly signal to him the result of the war but when he heard that The Duke of Wellington had won, he reputedly put out the rumour that Napoleon had won, causing markets to crash, which allowed him to snap up a great many family owned businesses that had been built up by hard work and risk over generations, all for next to nothing.

Something like this could only happen in a democratic system without a strong core code. Any noble who did something like this in a system with a strong core code would be severely punished and stripped of his titles. Such actions might not have been strictly illegal in the past but how could any just society tolerate the absolute dishonour of such an action?

Astonishingly, democracy does little to protect itself or its people against this sort of deceit.

A legitimate business ruse some might say but deception is the very heart of evil. If it was not a crime, it should have been.

The hard-won generational fortunes of hundreds of families were wiped out in one morning and a vast new power was gained by someone who was willing to use deceit destructively. In this we might see explanations for many of our current problems.

Many people believe there is a strong activist influence behind the machinations of modern Globalist communism. It also must be said that if these activists are successful in achieving the goals they set out to, it is because they have a clear sense of what they wish to achieve and because they are strongly unified in the achievement of those goals.

We cannot achieve our goals by vilifying others in generalizing ways when only a very few of any particular ethnic groups may be instrumental in trying to achieve our downfall yet we also cannot achieve our own goals if we do not unite in the cause of promoting them.

The fact is, above all else, we should learn the lesson of unity from those who use it successfully. The goals of our enemies seem to be clear and a good many of them work together effectively to achieve them. Shall we idly stand by then, while enemies engineer our slow and painful demise?

To finalize this appeal, I am obliged to shock you deeply with a quote from Robin Bruce Lockhart's work in 'Reilly, Ace of Spies, where he describes the horrors of the first few years of Bolshevik rule.

It might seem far-fetched that things like this could ever happen in the west but the fact is we are already experiencing the advanced warning signs of such evil repression in such things as vaccination mandates, toxic food and medicines and involvement in wars that we have not approved.

I quote:

'Dispatches reaching the (British) Foreign Office spoke of the operations of the Cheka (started and run initially by the Pole Felix Dzershinskii) as "making the history of the French Revolution and the Spanish Inquisition mild by comparison." Photographs were unprintable.

'By the hundreds and by the thousands, innocent people were tortured and murdered with unbelievable cruelty. The Communists would first strip the victims of their clothes, break their arms and legs, gouge out their eyes and cut off some fingers or a hand before stabbing them all over with a bayonet and smashing in their skulls with hatchets. Men would have their testicles cut off and many women and even school-girls under the age of ten had first to submit to rape.

'Other despatches to the foreign office told of people having their mouths slit by bayonets and their tongues cut out. Ex-Tsarist officers by the hundred had their shoulder straps nailed to their bodies then, bound naked in barbed wire they would be lowered naked into holes made in the ice until they froze to death. Countless others were burned alive, buried alive, thrown into wells to drown or placed in slag gas pits to die of suffocation. Luckier victims were shot or decapitated with a sword. Beards were torn from faces with the flesh on them, hot needles thrust under finger nails. Noses were cut off. Some victims were literally sawn in pieces and given to the dogs in the street to eat. Even the sick and the wounded were taken from hospitals to be hacheted to death. In Petrograd the canals were full of decomposed bodies and in one month the population of the city fell by 100,000. The situation elsewhere in Russia was little better. Even peasants were murdered when they protested at the requisition of their cattle. Factory workers were shot if they complained about conditions.

'Criminals had been loosed from the gaols and made commissars. In the prisons, innocent, starved and terrorized men, women and young girls were herded together in verminous, ill-ventilated cells with no sanitation. No one was allowed out except when called for execution.

'In Odessa, several hundred officers of the Black Sea Fleet had either been half killed in boiling steam and then drowned in the sea or tied to planks and pushed inch by inch into the ships furnaces. The crew of the Bolshevik flagship replaced their officers by taking on board the entire inmates of the two largest brothels in the port.

'In some districts in Russia, women were actually nationalized for the benefit of the comrades. A commissar would be given a certificate giving "the right to acquire a girl for himself and no one may oppose this in any way". Mixed schools were instituted in which pupil "commissars' sacked their masters and morals disintegrated so completely that venereal disease spread rapidly throughout Russia's school children.

'To reinforce this ghastly reign of terror, disease took a heavy toll of the population. The Red Guards rarely buried their victims but left them to rot where they lay. Typhus, cholera and smallpox were rife.

'It is hardly surprising that the main bulk of the people were anti-Bolshevik, but Lenin's policy was not only to break the spirit of the masses by terrorism but, by starvation, to break them in body as well. Those who were not committed Bolsheviks were only allowed a daily ration of one quarter pound of black bread or a half pound of unmilled oats. The starving people were physically incapable of throwing off the yoke of their better fed oppressors.'

***

Surely the minds behind Russian Bolshevism cannot have been human. Such things inspired me to write two different novel series exploring the possibility of covert alien control of human societies. It might be true and it might not be but could we in Western Europe, the UK, the USA, Canada, Australia and New Zealand be heading unwitting towards this sort of vile, demonic abuse down the track? I'm sure that nobody expected it in Russia, which for the most part had long been a civilised and forbearing society.

Many of the Bolsheviks themselves had been imprisoned more than once by the Czarist administration but were not tortured, starved or otherwise mistreated. They were generally released fairly quickly again only to continue planning their takeover with all the subsequent horrors and depredations.

Maybe things will not openly get as bad as they did in Bolshevik Russia, here, but we have to face the fact that cold, heartless communist opportunists are likely behind the slow yet sure degradation that has been going on in our societies for decades.

If so, it is safe to assume, given that they have poisoned us mentally and physically for years, that they are aiming at our total subjugation and or destruction.

Of course they aim to defeat us. If we do nothing, we condemn ourselves.

We desperately need a new order of knights like the Templars to guide us and protect us from evil.

We must act in our own self defence.

Only a fool ignores the truth.

Bibliography

Asimov, Isaac, Asimov Guide to the Physical Sciences, Pelican Books, New York, 1972

Berne, Eric, The Games People Play, Penguin, Harmondsworth, 1968

Bowen, James and Hobson, Peter, Theories of Education, Wiley, Gladesville, 1974

Brecht, Bertolt, Life of Galileo, (John Willett trans), Methuen, London, 1980

Brennan, JH, Experimental Magic, The Aquarian Press, Northamptonshire, 1972

Brennecke, Jochen, The Tirpitz, Horwitz, London, 1968

Buck, William, Mahabharata, Mentor, New York, 1973

Buck, William, Ramayana, Mentor, New York, 1976

Castaneda, Carlos, The Teachings of Don Juan, Penguin, Harmondsworth, 1970

Creighton, Christopher, (John Ainsworth-Davis), Op JB, Simon and Schuster, 1996

Dawkins, Richard, The Blind Watchmaker, Penguin, Harmondsworth, 1988

Dengate, Sue, Different Kids, Random House, Sydney, 1994

Dennison, George, The Lives of Children, Random House, New York, 1969

Duke, Dr David, My Awakening, Free Speech Press, Mandeville, 2008

Evola, Julius, The Doctrine of Awakening, Inner Traditions International, Rochester, 1996

Frazer, JG, The Golden Bough, Macmillan, London, 1960

George, Henry, Progress and Poverty, Kegan Paul, Trench & Co, London, 1884

Gibbon, Edward, Decline & Fall of the Roman Empire, Folio Society, London, 1985 (1776)

Griffin, G Edward, World Without Cancer, American Media, Westlake Village, 1974

Harding, James, The Duke of Wellington, International Profiles, London, 1969

Herodotus, The Histories, Penguin, Harmondsworth, 1972

Horne, Ross, Health and Survival in the 21st Century, Margaret Gee Publishing, Sydney 1992

Holy Scriptures, New World Translation, New York, 1984

Holy Scriptures, New World Translation, New York, 2013

Huxley, Aldous, Heaven and Hell, Penguin, Harmondsworth, 1959

Illich, Ivan, De-schooling Society, Penguin, Harmondsworth, 1973

Kingsley, Peter, In the Dark Places of Wisdom, The Golden Sufi Centre, Point Reyes, 1999

Klier, John and Mingay, Helen, Quest for Anastasia, Smith Gryphon, London, 1995

Knoke, Heinz, I Flew for the Fuhrer, Henry Holt and Company, New York, 1954

Laurence, TE, The Seven Pillars of Wisdom, Jonathan Cape, London, 1940

Legge, James (translator), The I Ching, Dover, New York, 1963

Lindsay, AD, Plato and Xenophon Socratic Discourses, JM Dent, London, 1910

Lockhart, Robin Bruce, Reilly Ace of Spies, Futura, London, 1983

Longford, Elizabeth, The Years of the Sword, Harper and Rowe, New York, 1969

Mahesh, Maharishi, On the Bhagavad Gita, Penguin, Harmondsworth, 1967

Mason, Colin, A Short History of Asia, Palgrave Macmillan, Basingstoke, 2014

Mason, Colin, A Short History of the Future, Earthscan, London, 2006

Mason, Mark, In Search of the Loving God, Dwapara Press, Eugene, 1997

Napoleon Bonaparte, The Code Napoleon, William Benning, London, 1827

Pavic, Milorad, Dictionary of the Khazars, Hamish, London, 1691

Pierce, Joseph Chiltern, Magical Child, Bantam, New York, 1977

Ponting, Clive, Churchill, Sinclair-Stevenson. London, 1994

Scheibner, Viera, Dr, Vaccinations, Scheibner, Blackheath, 1993

Shapiro, Max, The Penniless Billionaires, Times Books, New York, 1980

Smith, Huston, The Religions of Man, Perennial Library, New York, 1965

Speer, Albert, Inside the Third Reich, Macmillan, New York, 1970

The Holy Bible, King James, Odhams Press Ltd, London

The Holy Bible, NIV, Zondervan, Michigan, 1984

Thucydides, The Peloponnesian Wars, Washington Square Press, New York, 1963

Tzu, Sun, The Art of War (Denma Translation), Shambhala, Massachusetts, 2003

Villiers, Alan, Captain Cook, Penguin, Harmondsworth, 1969

Von Daniken, Erich, According to the Evidence, Book Club Associates, London, 1978

Watson, Lyall, Gifts of Unknown Things, Coronet, London, 1977

Woodham-Smith, Cecil, The Great Hunger, Four Square, London, 1965

Yeager, General Chuck and Janos, Leo, Yeager, Arrow, London, 1986

Index